Integrated Thematic Units

Amy E. Seely, M.Ed.

Teacher Created Materials, Inc.

Cover Design by Darlene Spivak

Made in U.S.A.
ISBN 1-55734-840-5
Order Number TCM 840

Table of Contents

Introduction

Integrated Thematic Units discusses possibilities for implementing an integrated curriculum approach in the classroom. Chapters highlight such issues as the historical beginnings of integrated curriculum and learning, classroom environments, initial steps toward an integrated curriculum approach in your classroom, two common approaches to integration of concepts, and assessment strategies. Throughout the chapters, examples are provided to support the ideas and perspectives of an integrated curriculum approach in the classroom. Sample forms are also included to help you begin thinking about ways in which integrated learning may be implemented in your classroom.

As you read the chapters, I hope you will begin to understand the complexities and dynamic nature of integrated learning. Within an integrated curriculum approach, students are encouraged to view learning as a process with many different pathways to knowledge. *Integrated Thematic Units* offers you an opportunity to reflect on the learning process and strategies for expanding connections and links between ideas and concepts.

Beginnings:
A Preview to Integration

What Is an Integrated Curriculum Approach?

Imagine walking into an elementary school classroom where students are actively participating and working on a myriad of tasks. In one area of the room you see students reading a trade book. In another, students are working with a recipe, trying to increase the ingredient amount by four because of the number of people in their class. Meanwhile, a group of students have just returned from outside where they were collecting leaf samples from the school grounds. This group is planning to use the leaves for a comparing/contrasting activity. The teacher, while at first difficult to see, is sitting down with a fourth group of students, listening to their discussion about mood and aesthetic response to the paintings they created. As you look around the room you begin to notice the arrangement of desks, in clusters rather than rows. The students are talking with each other as they work. The walls have a variety of student-created samples, including charts, graphs, pictures, and even work-in-progress samples. Additionally, there are many items in the classroom brought in from home, the community, and other resources. From your brief moment in this classroom, there appears to be a

> Imagine walking into an elementary school classroom where students are actively participating and working on a myriad of tasks.

1

connection between all the activities and tasks the students are working on. Upon leaving the classroom you have a sense that what the students are working on is important and relevant. What you have just imagined is not uncommon or impossible. It is an approach to curriculum and learning that is revolutionizing how students construct meaning about the world around them. This approach has many names—integrated thematic units, integrated curriculum, thematic teaching, theme study, and learning across the curriculum.

An integrated thematic unit approach to learning and teaching is a pathway for learners and teachers to construct meaningful connections between the classroom world and the world at large. As students participate in an integrated thematic unit, their own experiences and knowledge about the world are incorporated into the classroom activities. The classroom becomes a "window on the world" (Shubert, 1993). No longer are concepts and facts presented in an isolated, decontextualized manner with little relevance to the lives of students. Rather, there is an emphasis on meaning making, problem solving, and discovery. Students are active participants in the classroom, constructing and building connections between ideas and concepts they already know and new ideas and concepts they are being introduced to. As the connections are created, the integrated curriculum approach "represents a way to avoid the fragmented and irrelevant acquisition of isolated facts, transforming knowledge into personally useful tools for learning new information" (Lipson, Valencia, Wixon, & Peters, 1993, p. 252).

The approach taken with an integrated curriculum is one that makes explicit the ways in which connections between ideas are perceived. Concepts and facts presented in one area of the curriculum, for example, language arts, are not separated from those learned in other content areas, like social studies and science. In most instances, a unifying theme undergirds the connection. The theme is approached from many different angles, each one having a connection to the others. So, if a classroom was focusing on the theme of "Harvest Time," the literature may include stories from various cultures on celebrations and festivals related to harvest time. Science activities may focus on the types of vegetables found during the fall and the changes in the leaves during this time of year. In social studies, the students may be discussing the various celebrations being read about in the literature books. Throughout the activities, the students are engaged in various writing tasks that promote the learning and integration of ideas.

Upon leaving the classroom you have a sense that what the students are working on is important and relevant.

2

The Origination of Integrated Curriculum

The integrated curriculum approach is not new to the field of education. The perspectives and ideas of this approach have been around since the days of John Dewey (1933) and progressive education. Even before this movement, however, there were rumblings of the importance of providing students with curriculum that was correlated and connected. Herbart, a German philosopher, was influential in promoting these ideas in American education in the late 1890's. For him, correlation involved the interlinking of different ideas from different subjects. Concepts presented in one area of the curriculum can be linked with ideas in other parts of the curriculum, thereby establishing a correlation between the two or more subjects. The process of interlinking and correlating ideas across content areas enables students to unite experiences and generalize knowledge.

In accordance with Herbart's ideas, Dewey and his colleagues during the progressive education era were committed to ideas presented in an integrated curriculum approach to learning and teaching. The writings in the early 1930's about school reform, the process of reflective thought, and curriculum development discussed the importance of constructing knowledge through associations and relationships. Integration can occur only in and through a pathway of associations (Dewey & Childs, 1933). Associations are made as thoughts are connected together in a coherent manner. These associations are many and diverse. Dewey held to the belief that in order to understand the meaning of a thing, an event, or a situation, one must perceive it in relation to other things: how it works, what causes it, what the consequences are that follow it, and what uses it can be put to (Dewey, 1933). The significance of the relationships established between concepts is what is important to learning. As students begin to recognize the associations, they will discover that there is more to understanding ideas and concepts than merely being acquainted with the activities (Hullfish, 1933). Understandings and knowledge are developed as students make sense of the world through their experiences.

Dewey's work also emphasized the idea that school is a socializing agent and that students gain knowledge through shared, cooperative activities. Education is the process of social interaction (Dewey & Childs, 1933). By engaging in cooperative activities, students develop understandings about the ways of the world and how to function within the society. Learning develops as a result of participating in shared endeavors. The social nature of education and learning is promoted in an integrated curriculum where students are

> The process of interlinking and correlating ideas across content areas enables students to unite experiences and generalize knowledge.

3

encouraged to participate in shared activities, discovering associations and connections between ideas and concepts.

Along with the view of constructing associations between concepts, there was also the prevailing belief among those in the progressive education movement that education was to educate the whole child. Principles guiding this movement included such ideas as direct experience and problem solving as children develop individually and as participants in society (Good, 1956). There was a focus on creating stimulating environments and allowing students to follow their own interests. Classrooms were to be rich in materials and full of opportunities for initiative and self-expression. "The learner's ideas must be self-grown, his actions must ring true to the qualities of his own nature" (Thayer, 1933, p. 229). Students were free to explore their own desires, with interest being the primary motivater. Many of the activities and experiences promoted in the curriculum were to reflect experiences found outside of the classroom, such as learning about plant and animal life and the workings of a farm. "Only when [students] can talk, work, explore, and make things, can they truly live and grow" (Good, 1956, p. 360).

> Over the years, the classroom picture has changed with the times, but the basic ideas have remained the same.

Curricula has been in a constant state of change since the beginnings of public school. Sometimes the changes occur slowly, other times radically. The ideas and perspectives undergirding the integrated curriculum approach are not novel ideas to the education front. Rather, these thoughts have been around for close to one hundred years. Over the years, the classroom picture has changed with the times, but the basic ideas have remained the same. Concepts and subjects are not taught in isolation but as an integrated whole. Students are encouraged to bring in their own experiences and background knowledge to make the relevant connections between the classroom world and the world at large. "Learning is the reconstruction and reorganization of experience" (Thayer, 1933, p. 229). Students are able to share their experiences with others in collaborative settings. There is an emphasis on group work and collaboration. These basic premises have continued on as significant characteristics, defining an integrated curriculum approach to learning and teaching.

The Resurgence of Integrated Curriculum

Knowing that integrated learning is not revolutionary to the educational front, there has been a recent resurgence of popularity in classrooms throughout the country. There are more teachers implementing an integrated learning and teaching approach through thematic units to develop knowledge and understandings in their students. The resurgence has come about for many reasons, including the recognition that learners in our classrooms come from culturally diverse backgrounds and a revisited look at the social constructivism philosophy of learning and thinking. In past years, literacy events taking place in the classroom setting often mirrored those most commonly associated with mainstream homes (i.e., European-American and/or middle class). Literacy practices in mainstream settings generally involve the bedtime story routine, exposure to print, such as signs, billboards, posters, etc., with explicit ways of talking about the texts, and a belief that written literacy is a highly valuable practice. The classroom, then, was a place to continue developing literacy practices that were aligned with the home setting. However, the demographics in our country and schools are changing, with students coming from many different ethnic and cultural backgrounds. The U. S. Department of Education (1993) reports that between 1985 and 1992 the enrollment of limited-English-proficient students in public schools increased by fifty-six percent. By the year 2020, the number of students who speak a language other than English will increase from two million to five million (Nieto, 1992). With this increase in culturally diverse students, the pathways to knowledge and literacy development must also reflect this diversity. Research indicates that learners from nonmainstream homes bring diverse experiences and ways to represent those experiences to the classroom (Heath, 1983; Dyson, 1995). Through these diverse representations about the world, knowledge is shared and expanded to include many perspectives and points of view. An integrated curriculum approach to learning fosters and supports the many ways in which learners interpret and share meanings among those in the classroom community.

Knowledge is constructed by making connections between past and present experiences.

A social constructive perspective to thinking and learning emphasizes the social nature of development as well as the idea that learning occurs as a process. Knowledge is constructed by making connections between past and present experiences. These experiences are generated through the social interactions learners engage in. As students participate in activities within the classroom environment, new meanings are explored and shared. The impact of these negotiations leads to new ways of thinking and viewing the world.

Social constructivism emerged as a philosophy through the writings and beliefs of Vygotsky (1978) and others who have modified and adapted his views, such as Bruner (1986), Rogoff (1990), and Dyson (1993). The underlying premise of social constructivism is that all thought is social in nature. It is through social interactions with others that learners come to their own understandings about how the world operates. They grapple with their new knowledge as past

5

experience is integrated with present information. This development of knowledge is dependent upon the social context of the event, the actions and changes learners experience. The learning process and the social context in which it happens are embedded within each other. Rogoff (1990) adds to the discussion by saying, "context is not so much a set of stimuli that impinge upon a person as it is a web of relations interwoven to form the fabric of meaning" (p. 27). The uniqueness of a learner's experiences contributes to the myriad of pathways of development that emerge. Learning is then perceived as a socially constructed process.

Expanding on the social constructivist perspective of learning and thinking, an integrated learning approach exploits the web of relations discovered while participating in activities and tasks. Integration of concepts and ideas follows on the heels of whole-language views and process-oriented approaches to literacy development. Goodman (1989) discusses how the integration of oral and written language leads to the development of thinking. Language, according to proponents of whole language, is inherently integrative and should be approached as such. Meaning is developed when the language processes of speaking, listening, reading, and writing are kept whole, not fragmented. Additionally, learners engaged in whole-language events are provided opportunities to create meaning through relevant, authentic contexts. Reading and writing events are seen as purposeful and necessary for something. With the process-oriented approach to literacy development, learning is not assumed to be linear and sequential, but involves a variety of paths and explorations (Applebee, 1991). Students actively create meaning through various texts, encouraging integration and connections among ideas. The focus for process-oriented activities is the thinking process that learners engage in while constructing meaning. Whole-language views and process-oriented approaches to literacy development support the integration of ideas in the classroom.

> **Integration of concepts and ideas follows on the heels of whole language views and process-oriented approaches to literacy development.**

In addition to literacy development, the interest in problem-solving approaches in mathematics and the discovery approach to science have impacted the surge of the integrated curriculum approach to learning. Social constructivist thinking also underlies problem-solving and discovery. Learners are provided opportunities to build pathways of exploration and solutions. They are encouraged to work in a social context, negotiating and reshaping their interpretations of the world. The problem-solving approach emphasizes open-ended problems with many solutions. In science, students are encouraged to participate in hands-on activities. Integrating ideas and concepts throughout the curriculum promotes problem-solving and discovery approaches. Students come to view the relevance and authenticity of mathematics and science in real situations, as opposed to memorizing facts.

The resurgence of the integrated curriculum approach to learning and thinking is, therefore, coming about as teachers and educators develop understandings about the social constructivist perspective of learning, including whole-language views, process-oriented thinking patterns, problem solving, and discovery. Recognizing the impact of culturally diverse learners and their development has also increased interest in integrated thematic units to develop learning and thinking. Teachers and students are exploring new pathways to knowledge. As the learning process unfolds, learners integrate their knowledge, leading to newly constructed representations. The social nature of learning embodies the belief that learning involves sharing culture and knowledge with others (Bruner, 1986).

Ideas Within Ideas

An integrated thematic unit approach to learning and thinking provides teachers and educators with a view of a curriculum that is overlapping and interacting, rather than a series of separate concentric circles with common centers. A nested view perceives learning and relationships as occurring in and among various contexts. The relationships established are constructed through multiple pathways, each one interacting and transacting with the others. As learners participate in learning tasks, knowledge is connected to other ideas and contexts. The context both situates and shapes the curriculum, encompassing subject matter and social organization and their interrelations (Cornbleth, 1990). Subject matter includes personal, social, and world knowledge, while the social organization involves teacher and student roles and patterns of interaction. For example, learning about the industrial revolution might incorporate discussions about machinery and systems, the benefits and problems, as well as a discussion about the ways in which society has reacted to the changes. Teachers and students engage not in a transmission mode of learning, a one-way pattern of interaction where one transmits ideas and knowledge to those passively receiving the knowledge, but rather a transactive model where dialogues of ideas are shared and developed. Through an integrated curriculum approach, learners and teachers are able to explore and shape contexts for learning. "The focus is on what knowledge and learning opportunities actually are made available to students, how they are created, and what values they reflect and sustain" (Cornbleth, 1990, p. 25).

Nested contexts within the curriculum offer learners opportunities to construct knowledge in a myriad of interesting ways. Learners are able to reflect on their own experiences in other contexts to make

> As the learning process unfolds, learners integrate their knowledge, leading to newly constructed representations.

sense of the newly presented ideas and concepts. The many contexts in which learning occurs are interactive and nested within each other. A context or environment used in one situation may be connected and used in another learning situation.

Concluding Remarks

Having a bit of the history and reasons for the resurgence of the integrated curriculum approach to learning provides a framework to begin thinking about the benefits and importance of integrating the curriculum implemented in your classroom. Learners come to activities and tasks with their own experiences and background to guide them. Through social interaction and participation, knowledge is constructed and negotiated among those in the learning community. The newly developed understandings are reflected in the ways in which learners perceive and interact with the world. As you continue to explore the dimensions of integrated learning and integrated curriculum approaches to teaching, you will encounter alternative ways of thinking about teaching and learning. An integrated approach to learning and curriculum development enables students and teachers to participate in new dialogues and pathways to learning. Shifts in thinking and learning patterns emerge, providing an integrated, relevant curriculum where meaning is constructed and purposeful to the lives of students.

Classrooms That Support Integrated Learning

No More Disengaged Students

Recall the scenario described in the opening of the first chapter. The setting has changed considerably from the days of a transmission mode of teaching where teachers are lecturing to passive students sitting in rows. Rather, the environment reflects active students, generally in groups of four to six, working on a variety of tasks. The teacher often moves around the classroom, listening to students as they explore and investigate important concepts. The setting appears less structured, yet the students are more involved and motivated. The activities are interesting and relevant to the students. Now you may be asking, what connection is there between this type of classroom environment and integrated curriculum? Isn't it possible to have this learning environment and not integrate content areas? The answer is yes, you can create this type of learning environment without integrating the curriculum. The point here is to consider ways in which the environment can influence the curriculum. Integrating the curriculum will not only provide overall coherence, but will support the atmosphere you have initially created. Encouraging students to formulate understandings from a variety of

> Integrating the curriculum will not only provide overall coherence, but will support the atmosphere you have initially created.

perspectives enables them to develop connections and associations between and among concepts and contexts.

Environments that support integrated learning and integrated thematic units have common features about them. These common features involve not only the arrangement of desks and activities but also a variety of interactional styles between participants in the classroom and a perspective that teachers, as well as students, are continuous learners and researchers. The most common features found in classrooms that implement an integrated curriculum include cooperative learning activities, alternative interactional patterns, flexibility and balance, a solid understanding of concepts and skills addressed, and teachers who consistently perceive themselves as reflective learners of new ideas.

Cooperative Learning

Cooperative learning is a common practice implemented in integrated curriculum classrooms. Cooperative learning is a process whereby learners are encouraged to work together to discover solutions and meanings. The discovery promotes negotiations, in that the students come to activities with diverse experiences and knowledge bases. Negotiations offer students opportunities to reconsider, reevaluate, and reshape ideas and concepts to help explain and clarify their thinking patterns. As your students participate in cooperative activities, they become familiar with the many perspectives and ideas their peers bring to the learning situation.

Cooperative learning activities provide your students with opportunities to participate in social interactions. Discussed earlier in the section on social constructivism, knowledge is not only developed through the text but also in the context of social interaction. Reflecting on the thoughts of Vygotsky (1978) and other social constructivists, students develop and expand their understandings about the world around them through the collaboration with more capable peers. More informed students can encourage their peers to consider other ideas and rethink prior knowledge. This leads to negotiations and new interpretations. Collaborative learning activities generally promote achievement and productivity because your students have a greater sense of security knowing they can interact with others to affirm ideas and solve problems. They are sources of information for each other as they work together.

Teachers implementing cooperative learning activities in their classrooms utilize a variety of grouping strategies to maximize learning potential. In some situations you select students for the groups; other times the students self-select their groups. Groups are configured for a variety of purposes. You might be interested in having students develop oral language skills, in which case you may group quiet students together with a predetermined topic and expectations to encourage discussion and participation. Other times you may be interested in observing how students negotiate their ideas on controversial topics and in noting the group dynamics that arise. Or you may want students to help each other modify and extend interpretations (Leal, 1993). Regardless of the grouping, the underlying goal is having students work together in a constructive, productive environment.

Cooperative learning activities emphasize the importance of shared responsibility for group projects. In any group, individual students are responsible for various aspects of the task. It is only through the cooperation and participation of each member that the project is successful. Many teachers have job cards for students. These jobs are assigned either weekly or in accordance with the tasks and activities. In a grouping of four, there might be a leader, a monitor, a recorder, and a reporter. The leader is responsible for initiating the discussion or asking the group for ideas. The monitor's responsibility is to insure all voices are heard and that the discussion is progressing forward. Recorders write down the ideas and solutions. Finally, the reporter is responsible for disseminating the information to other groups and class members. In assigning roles and jobs, all students are able to participate in the group and have some level of responsibility to the group and the project. Cooperative learning promotes social interaction and shared responsibility among learners, leading to new interpretations about the world.

Regardless of the grouping, the underlying goal is having students work together in a constructive, productive environment.

Alternative Interactional Patterns

Along with cooperative learning activities, an integrated approach to knowledge and thinking encourages diverse interactional patterns among those in the classroom community. Students and teachers are interacting with each other in a variety of ways on many different levels. This appears to be quite different from even a decade ago when the focus was on a transmission model of teaching.

In a transmission model of teaching, the classroom interactional pattern consists of what has been termed IRE—initiate, respond, evaluate pattern (Mehan, 1979). In this pattern, the teacher initiates dialogue by calling on a student to share or respond; the student responds; and the teacher provides some sort of evaluative comment before progressing further. The dialogue is generally not open-ended and problem-solving in nature, but rather the teacher elicits a factual, single-right-answer response. The dialogue, or discourse, and participation are dominated by the teacher. She/he selects the student to offer the response. With the IRE structure, students rarely have the opportunity to initiate discussions or even contribute to the discussion beyond what the teacher had originally conceived. There is little room for flexibility and movement within the discourse. The IRE pattern of classroom interaction presents a view of teachers owning all the information and students passively receiving the knowledge via presentations and lectures. The IRE structure of interaction does not provide many opportunities for learners to share and negotiate their interpretations.

Establishing alternative interactional patterns in the classroom setting involves you and your students viewing the learning process as dialogic and collaborative. Teachers and learners engage in meaning construction through listening and responding to others' ideas and thoughts. Incorporated within these dialogues are each other's responses, providing spaces to build new understandings (Dyson, 1993). The interactional patterns of the classroom become flexible and diverse as students and teachers contribute their own knowledge and experiences to the dialogues. Following are some questions to ask as you incorporate a collaborative model of teaching into your classroom:

Teachers and learners engage in meaning construction through listening and responding to others' ideas and thoughts.

◆ How do I share my expertise and knowledge with my students?

◆ How can I foster students' development of knowledge?

◆ How do I incorporate voices of students who may come from a range of backgrounds and have different interactional patterns?

◆ How do I enable students to hear and respond to other voices and beliefs?

Along with small and large group discussions, debates, and partner sharing, peer group discussions offer you and your students an alternative platform for collaborative interaction. When students, rather than the teacher, are catalysts for discussions, personal and authentic purposes for learning are encouraged. Peer group discussions provide "opportunities for students to explore meaning together, creating and investigating new possibilities for interpretation" (Leal, 1993, p. 117). In all grades, student-initiated discussion enables students to explore ideas and thoughts in a supportive atmosphere, one less threatening than if the teacher had initiated the discussion. Primary grade teachers have a greater role in facilitating discussions. Younger students often need modeling of how to participate in discussions. Older students may require less modeling, and the teacher's role is to insure all voices are heard and respected. Additionally, the peer group discussion promotes student responsibility and ownership for learning. Students are more motivated and engaged, knowing the discussions are initiated and mediated by them. They view themselves as resources for information.

The transference of responsibility creates opportunities for the teacher to assess and evaluate students' understandings of the ideas and concepts. You are able to reflect on the learning process and provide further clarification and instruction when necessary. Peer group discussions give you a window through which you can view students' prior knowledge and the connections and associations they are creating. The information gathered from listening and observing students in peer group discussions is beneficial to both students and teachers as meaning is constructed in an integrated curriculum.

Alternative interactional patterns to learning and thinking enable you and your students to become responsive, reflective participants. Opening up the classroom to include diverse interactional patterns encourages students to make significant and meaningful connections between their own ideas, peers' ideas, and ideas from the world around them. Alternative interactional patterns, which emphasize collaboration, provide a platform for uniting the cognitive and social aspects of learning (Cazden, 1988).

Flexibility and Balance

An important feature found in integrated curriculum classrooms is flexibility. Students bring to any learning situation their own experiences and prior knowledge. As ideas are negotiated and meanings reinterpreted, diversions are expected to occur. Students participating in peer group discussions or other alternative interactional structures will bring into the discussion ideas and thoughts that are of great interest to them. It is impossible for any one teacher to predict the thoughts of students and what course the discussion will take. While routines and patterns are important to the instructional day, sensitivity to students' needs and interests should guide the schedule. Opportunities to explore and expand on various ideas of interest are more readily available in classrooms implementing integrated curricula.

Flexibility is important as your students actively participate and construct their own interpretations and representations about the world. With the flexibility to follow diversions, there is a sense of freedom in trying to balance and attend to all areas of the curriculum. Integrated thematic units enable teachers and students to focus on specific content areas without worrying that the balance has been

> While routines and patterns are important to the instructional day, sensitivity to students' needs and interests should guide the schedule.

disrupted. During one topic or unit the focus might be on social studies; another time it might be on science. It is not of concern to teachers or students because the balance will shift at another time (Gamberg, Kwak, Hutchings, & Altheim, 1988). The balance of content areas, while not apparent in the daily instruction, is a part of the overall schedule. For example, a class might be studying the historical perspective of American colonists in the late 1780's and compare them to present-day life styles. This topic is one that lends itself more heavily to social studies. Later in the year the class might delve into the workings of the human body with a science-oriented perspective on studying cells and systems. While the focus of the material might be heavy in one content area, it does not exclude the others. The nature of an integrated curriculum approach is to bring in as many perspectives as possible, while maintaining relevance and authenticity. The balance of content areas is maintained over the course of the school year.

> **The balance of content areas, while not apparent in the daily instruction, is a part of the overall schedule.**

As you integrate the curriculum and think about ideas as units and topics, learning is perceived as a whole, occurring over the entire year rather than as isolated pieces of information taught in a random fashion. Flexibility to include alternative pathways to learning and viewing the overall balance of content areas are inherent features in implementing a successful integrated curriculum in the classroom.

Solid Understandings of Concepts and Skills

Teachers implementing an integrated curriculum approach to learning should have a solid understanding of the concepts and skills students should become familiar with over the course of the instructional year. Being knowledgeable about the various skills and concepts is critical to successful teaching because of the diverse avenues your students may take to discover information.

As you implement an integrated curriculum, you will often create activities and tasks from a variety of sources. In pulling together different sources, you develop a meaning-centered integrated curriculum. State and district frameworks outline various skills and concepts in each of the content areas. The frameworks often present the information in global terms, with few specifics or ideas as to how to teach the information. The value of frameworks is they provide the overall picture for teachers to begin planning the curriculum and activities. Resource guides, including teacher editions of textbooks, are more detailed and offer suggestions and ideas. Teachers also gather information through colleagues and other educators. As you share and collaborate on ideas, skills and concepts are addressed. And finally, the best source to use in developing the curriculum is your students. Gathering information on their learning patterns and ways they approach tasks is the most helpful in creating a meaning-centered, integrated curriculum. By observing and assessing student participation and growth, you can develop activities and tasks that will best meet the needs of the students. These sources provide you with numerous avenues to take in addressing skills and concepts.

Integrating the curriculum, however, is more than pulling together sources and ideas under one general theme. When creating integrated instruction, it is important to keep in mind that activities and tasks should be selected and used because they promote educational value and progress. It is not enough to have the activities transcend subject matter lines (Brophy & Alleman, 1991). Often activities are included that provide a false sense of integration, such as pluralizing nouns in a social studies unit. This activity has value in language arts, but is not relevant to the ideas in social studies. Knowing grade level expectations and development provides you with a framework to utilize as you plan the curriculum. A meaningful and relevant curriculum is conceptualized when clear understandings of grade level concepts and skills are addressed in the activities and tasks.

> Integrating the curriculum, however, is more than pulling together sources and ideas under one general theme.

Teachers As Reflective Learners and Researchers

While it is recognized teachers should be knowledgeable about the content and concepts students are working with, an integrated thematic unit approach encourages teachers to search out more effective and diverse methods of instruction and teaching. Teachers are no longer seen as the only source of information. They perceive themselves not as owners and disseminators of information, but as receptors and learners of new knowledge. Teachers as learners are able to gather insights about their students, themselves, and their own teaching strategies. You bring to the curriculum your own interpretive frameworks for thinking (Pappas, Kiefer, & Levstick, 1995). Taking the perspective that there is no one right or single way to approach learning and thinking, implementing an integrated curriculum enables you to be open and receptive to the many avenues your students take to understand the world around them.

Reflective teachers understand that learning is complex and personal. Learners come to tasks on many levels with many experiences. The complexity of learning requires that teachers approach learning and teaching as uncertain processes (Henderson, 1992). These processes interact with each other based upon past and personal experiences. Reflection on these experiences impacts the connections and relationships established in new learning situations. As you reflect on yourself, your students, and your teaching strategies, you seek ways to make learning more meaningful by adapting and shaping the curriculum to meet the needs of the students (Henderson, 1992). Self-reflection opens the door to new possibilities and paradigms of teaching and thinking (Seely, 1994). An integrated curriculum approach with its philosophical stance in social constructivism and the social nature of learning, along with flexibility, provides opportunities for teachers to engage in reflection and inquiry. You are able to gain insights that might not otherwise be apparent in more structured, decontextualized curriculum.

Teachers who perceive themselves as learners continuously explore paths to increase the effectiveness of their teaching. They become researchers of their own practice. By thoughtfully examining their own actions and practices, teachers can reconsider and expand upon their ideas, leading to multiple paths of teaching and learning (Seely, 1994). These expanded views offer new possibilities for students. Teaching through an integrated curriculum approach encourages you to "decide ways of proceeding, to choose among alternative pathways, or to gain new understandings about yourself, the context of the situation, and your unquestioned assumptions about practice" (Graham, 1993, p. 34).

> Integrated curriculums also support teachers as they reflect on their teaching strategies and the effectiveness of the curriculum.

Concluding Remarks

Purposeful integrated curriculum approaches often have in place common features embedded within the environment that help support the meaningfulness and relevance of the integration. Within the classroom environment, teachers and students adopt alternative interactional patterns as they participate in cooperative and collaborative activities. These activities promote the social nature of learning and the perspective that learning is a constructed process. As students engage in the activities and tasks offering diverse thinking patterns and investigating uncharted pathways, the teachers have a sense of flexibility. The flexibility within integrated thematic units to explore new ideas is balanced by solid understandings and knowledge of the concepts and skills to be addressed. Integrated curriculums also support teachers as they reflect on their teaching strategies and the effectiveness of the curriculum. There is room within the curriculum to adjust and reconsider ideas and pathways, enabling you to be a learner and a researcher of your craft.

Developing Integrated Thematic Units

Initial Steps

An integrated thematic approach to learning and teaching is an approach that does not just occur at the wave of a magic wand. Integrating the curriculum and teaching through a thematic approach requires planning and vision. Planning units and themes to address important concepts throughout the year involves teachers and students in the decision process. An integral aspect of integrated learning is that teachers and students are able to explore ideas in many different ways. These alternative avenues generally do not come preplanned and packaged, but are constructed by the students' thinking patterns and interests. Knowing the connections are unique and varied among any group of learners, how does one get started in thinking about integrated curricula and integrated teaching? There are some beginning steps to take as you initiate and implement an integrated thematic approach to curriculum and learning. These beginning steps involve discovering and selecting themes to be implemented in the classroom, determining criteria for appropriateness of themes, and restructuring the instructional day to accommodate larger projects and activities inherent in integrated

> Integrating the curriculum and teaching through a thematic approach requires planning and vision.

thematic units. These steps are critical to the actualization of an integrated curriculum approach in your classroom.

Looking for Themes

The first step to take as one begins the road to integrated curriculum and thematic teaching is to identify sources of themes. Where do themes originate? How do teachers create meaningful topics to be used in thematic units? Beginning with the district and state curriculum frameworks, teachers identify the parameters of the study. There are many concepts and skills addressed at each grade level. Some teachers are mandated to follow a predetermined curriculum; others have more flexibility. Regardless of the freedom one has in planning, some concepts are better explored in certain thematic units than others. The use of themes in an integrated curriculum provides both an organizational tool for identifying learning objectives and a supportive context to construct meaningful and relevant knowledge (Rand, 1994). It is important to the success of integrated learning and thematic units that the teacher has a sense of the overall picture of student growth and development. The overall picture provides you and your students with parameters within which to work.

> **The first step to take as one begins the road to integrated curriculum and thematic teaching is to identify sources of themes.**

The teacher also takes into consideration the needs, interests, and developmental level of the students to help define the parameters (Smith & Johnson, 1994). To find out where your students might be in development and interests, the following questions may be considered:

- ◆ What do your students like to participate in?
- ◆ What activities do they seem to enjoy and get excited about?
- ◆ When do your students appear challenged and motivated, yet not frustrated?
- ◆ What are the topics of their conversations?

Answers to these questions provide a starting place as you begin developing lists of topics for integrated thematic units.

Once the parameters are defined, a list of possible themes is generated. The brainstorming list should include anything that is remotely possible. This activity is best achieved when other colleagues or students are involved. It is as though one person's thoughts provide the spark for someone else's ideas. When teachers include students in the brainstorming session, students begin to have a sense of ownership in the learning process. Ownership of the learning process enables students to have a voice in the process. There is a higher desire to learn when students are provided opportunities to participate in the planning process than when they must follow the paths prescribed by a teacher (Newkirk, 1991). Brainstorming with students also encourages them to gain an understanding of how themes and ideas are generated and teaches them those themes and ideas do not appear out of nowhere. The modeling process is especially helpful for students as they begin brainstorming their own lists for writing topics and other projects. Lists generated by you and/or your students and colleagues, therefore, serve a dual purpose—to involve your students in the learning process and to allow possible themes to emerge.

To help with brainstorming lists of ideas for themes, you may ask your students questions concerning special interests and talents:

◆ What do you do well in school? Out of school?

◆ What do you know a lot about in the classroom? Outside the classroom?

◆ What do you want to know more about? Learn to do better?

While brainstorming with colleagues and students is a valuable way to discover themes, you may also utilize other resources for ideas. There are many books available offering suggestions and ideas, from bibliographies of children's literature to specific thematic units already developed. Themes may also surface in teacher editions of textbooks. As you begin to think about teaching through an integrated thematic approach, an awareness of possibilities will become more apparent. Utilizing community and local resources is another avenue to explore when developing themes for the classroom. Community resources promote connections and relationships between the classroom and the world. Bringing in the wide variety of possibilities and potential ideas will aid you as you develop thematic units to implement in your classroom.

After generating a list of many ideas, the next step is to think about criteria to determine whether a theme is appropriate for your students and your classroom. Questions to consider include:

◆ Does this theme build upon my students' previous knowledge and experiences?

◆ Will this theme engage and interest my students for a length of time?

◆ What connections and relevance to the world around does this theme offer?

> Utilizing community and local resources is another avenue to explore when developing themes for the classroom.

The questions are meant to weed out themes that will not serve the desired purposes and intentions. Successful integrated thematic units must engage students and encourage relevant connections to the world. As you ask these questions and others you believe critical to the process, the list of themes is narrowed to only those that are true possibilities. This narrowed list of themes can then be disseminated to the group for a discussion or vote as to which one will be selected. Opening up the selection process to include students provides the sense of ownership and voice that promotes motivation and engagement.

Webs enable teachers and students to visualize ideas and potential connections between themes and content areas.

After a list of themes is generated, one method of brainstorming possible supporting activities for the theme is through a curriculum web (Rand, 1994). Webs enable teachers and students to visualize ideas and potential connections between themes and content areas. Placing ideas for themes into a web diagram "helps children link new learning to old and to organize mentally the information presented" (Rand, 1994, p. 180). A web diagram for themes has as the center focus the theme. Ideas and interests generated by you and your students frame the center, becoming possibilities. Curriculum webs can be as detailed as necessary. Samples of curriculum/planning webs are provided on the following pages.

Thus, as you and your students identify themes, you will participate in brainstorming sessions. Outside resources may be considered for ideas and topics that are relevant and interesting. Brought to the process are possibilities about what is interesting, motivating, and meaningful. It becomes a collaborative process whereby the voices of teachers and students are heard. Identifying and deciding on themes to pursue during the instructional year is an important step towards a meaningful, integrated curriculum approach to thinking and learning. Through thematic units and integrated learning, students "grow holistically without artificially compartmentalizing learning" (Rand, 1994, p. 178).

Planning Web

Use this form as a planning overview for thematic activities and assessments.

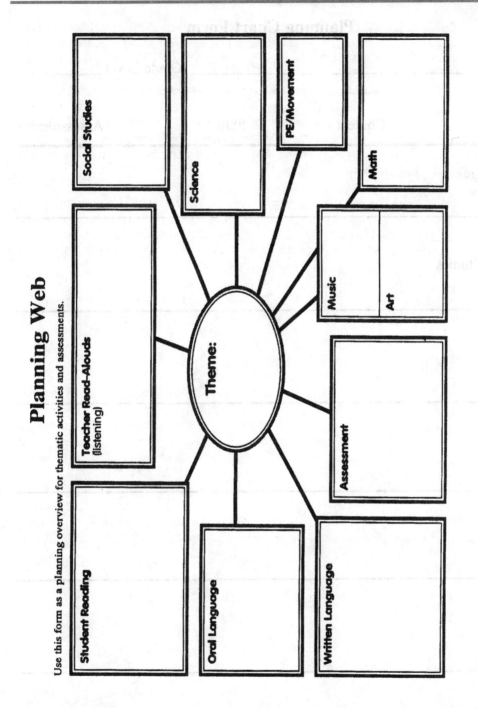

Reprinted from TCM Workshop Notebook Portfolios and Other Alternative Assessments, *Teacher Created Materials, 1993*

Planning Chart Form

Theme _____ Grade Level _____

Area	Content	Skill	Assessment
Language Arts			
Social Studies			
Math			
Science			
Art/Music			
Other			

Reprinted from TCM Workshop Notebook Portfolios and Other Alternative Assessments, *Teacher Created Materials, 1993*

Expanded Nature of Themes

Themes and units come in all shapes and sizes. Some are intensive and require the students' focus and time for weeks. Others are brief because students are interested for a limited time. As students participate in integrated learning they are exposed to various themes throughout their school careers. In many cases students in kindergarten and upper primary will be studying and exploring similar themes. The difference lies in the depth and breadth of the theme and instruction. For example, the theme of "growth and change" might be introduced to kindergarten students as they read *The Very Hungry Caterpillar* by Eric Carle (1967). The focus of the book is on how a caterpillar grows and changes into a butterfly. A discussion of how humans grow and change can follow. With the same theme of growth and change in the fifth grade, students may investigate population charts of their city and how the growth has affected the city in various ways, such as resources, crime, opportunities, etc. They may also discuss and explore the relationship between growth and change in science-related activities. The theme, while fully developed in a primary grade, is revisited in an upper grade with a different focus and intention. Integrated curricula offer many possibilities for teachers and students to revisit themes and units. As your students construct their own connections and thinking patterns, they follow many pathways, each time adding to and remembering different aspects of the theme. Students exposed to growth and change in kindergarten will recall various pieces of knowledge learned from *The Very Hungry Caterpillar* (Carle, 1967) as they investigate and create associations in a later grade utilizing the same theme with a new focus. With the overall theme remaining virtually the same throughout different grade levels, your task, then, is to discover and implement ideas that are best suited for the level of student interest and ability.

> The theme, while fully developed in a primary grade, is revisited in an upper grade with a different focus and intention.

The expanded nature of themes requires teachers to think about the appropriateness of the ideas generated from a theme. In most instances, themes cross boundaries and grade levels. To help facilitate the decision-making process, you can begin asking yourself the following questions (Shubert, 1993):

- ◆ Is it meaningful to my students?
- ◆ Does it have substance, and is it applicable to the real world that students live in?
- ◆ What connections can be fostered to apply to future themes?
- ◆ Is the theme broad enough, allowing room for skills and concepts to be included?

23

In asking these questions you may think about the relevance and importance of themes and units developed for classroom application. It is critical to the success of a unit that the overall theme is meaningful to students. Meaning resides in the interest and usefulness of the idea. Students actively engaged in activities and projects related to the theme will view the learning process as authentic and purposeful. Encouraging your students to participate in the planning of themes and units will help to create that interest. When students are involved in deciding their own pathways to learning, motivation and meaning are greatly increased. Opportunities for your students to participate in planning thematic units honors their voices and gives them a sense of empowerment. When students make decisions about what to learn and how to learn, they become personally invested and connected to the learning process. They link their learning activities with who they are, how they think, and what they care about (Oldfather, 1993).

> When students are involved in deciding their own pathways to learning, motivation and meaning are greatly increased.

With the sense of meaningfulness also comes relevance and authenticity to students' lives, both in and out of the classroom. Integrated thematic units are based on themes discovered in the world. Take, for example, the previous theme of growth and change. This theme is based on natural occurrences in the world. Students observe changes in many things as they begin to discover the world and their place within the world. Discovering changes and growth in plant and animal life, systems, weather, etc., provides students with information and knowledge about how the world operates. Bringing these ideas into the realm of the classroom encourages students to foster connections between the classroom and the world around. As these relationships and connections are developed, students are able to view the learning process as having relevance to their own lives. Connecting what is learned in the classroom and what is learned outside the classroom is accomplished through integrated thematic units.

As teachers develop integrated curricula that are meaningful to students, it is important to consider how connections to other themes might be fostered. Providing opportunities for students to create connections between and among themes and units supports the integrated nature of learning. As your students discover patterns of thinking, commonalties between bodies of knowledge become apparent. For example, students may come across a theme of "transitions" that has similarities to the earlier theme of growth and changes. Perhaps in transitions students discuss the idea of settling in a new land and the changes that occur. Utilizing knowledge acquired from growth and changes, students are able to construct meaningful connections to the new theme and concepts. Establishing relationships between thematic units provides learners with a greater sense of continuity in the learning process. This continuity supports the perspective that learning is more than an acquisition of isolated decontextualized facts; it is a process involving an integrated whole.

Important to the appropriateness of the theme is to consider whether it is broad enough to incorporate the multitude of skills required for the specific grade level. Students are expected to achieve a certain level of academic growth over the course of the instructional year, and teachers are expected to teach the required skills and concepts. As teachers begin to plan for integrated learning and thematic units, it should be remembered that students develop their thinking and knowledge through activities created within the theme and that an integrated curriculum does not add to an already overburdened curriculum. Integrated thematic units should be expansive and comprehensive, providing many avenues for connections to emerge. The activities and skills addressed in the thematic unit should be "natural extensions of the theme" (Lapp & Flood, 1994, p. 418). When planning thematic units, teachers match the necessary and important skills to engaging activities. Thus, to be a worthwhile endeavor, a thematic unit is comprehensive in addressing and teaching the skills and concepts identified in state and district frameworks as important to student growth and development.

An integrated curriculum approach to learning and teaching utilizes time differently than traditional curriculum.

Restructuring Time to Integrate the Curriculum

With themes and criteria for appropriateness in mind, another beginning step to address is the time factor. An integrated curriculum approach to learning and teaching utilizes time differently than traditional curriculum. Time in an integrated curriculum is divided, not into one-hour segments where a different content area is taught each hour, but into blocks of uninterrupted time, depending on the nature of the theme and the activities involved. An integrated curriculum strives to have students engaged in meaningful projects and activities, rather than the current reliance on unrelated small tasks.

Blocks of uninterrupted time are achieved when the instructional day is restructured. In many instances, the day is divided into two large blocks, one in the morning and one in the afternoon. Teachers who are just beginning to integrate the curriculum might focus on language arts in the morning and math/social sciences in the afternoon. As one becomes comfortable integrating the curriculum, the boundaries between blocks of time become more permeable, enabling the various content areas to be addressed throughout the instructional day. Restructuring the school day to include larger blocks of time to integrate the curriculum promotes the authenticity of learning. Learning occurs when time is not the controlling factor. Activities and projects should not be limited to one-hour time slots.

The best way to read a book, write a summary, or solve a problem is when interest and satisfaction are the determining factors. Incorporating uninterrupted blocks of time into the schedule encourages students to work on activities and projects until they are satisfied with the results and have moved on to other interests.

Providing your students with larger blocks of time throughout the instructional day recognizes the individuality of student growth and learning patterns. Not all students learn at the same pace. Requiring them to move through the curriculum and activities in the same amount of time denies the existence of differences in learners (Allington, 1994). Some students need more time to focus on and learn the concepts than the typically provided thirty to forty minutes of work time. Restructuring the day into larger blocks of time enables your students to have additional time and attention, if needed.

The complexity of projects and tasks in an integrated curriculum mirrors the real world.

In addition to recognizing individuality among learners, a restructured day encourages tasks and activities that are more complex and detailed in nature. Students are able to really delve into and participate in complicated activities, knowing they are not going to have to switch to another task or activity within the next thirty minutes or so. The complexity of projects and tasks in an integrated curriculum mirrors the real world. Outside of the classroom doors, problems do not come in isolated, neat packages with single answers, but rather are a complex web of possible solutions. Encouraging your students to think about situations in a similar fashion, presented in real world experiences, will promote the authenticity and relevance of learning.

Concluding Remarks

In this chapter, beginning steps towards an integrated curriculum approach to thinking and learning were discussed. These beginning steps include identifying themes, the appropriateness of these themes, and restructuring the instructional day into larger blocks of time. Identifying themes to implement in the classroom involves not only you but other colleagues and students. Participating in brainstorming sessions to generate ideas for themes and topics provides students and teachers with a sense of ownership and voice. The issue of appropriateness appears as you and your students consider the generated lists of ideas. Which theme is going to be meaningful and relevant to the lives of your students is an important question to ask and discuss. Restructuring the day to include large blocks of time supports the authenticity and individuality of learning and student development. These steps are critical to the success of implementing an integrated thematic approach to curriculum and learning.

Intradisciplinary Curriculum

Time to Consider Instruction

The classroom environment is ready. Students are working in cooperative groups, new interactional patterns are the norm rather than the exception, and the teacher is no longer the focal point of the classroom. The teacher views him/herself as a reflective learner and researcher, reconsidering and expanding on avenues to learning. Within the setting, you and your students have brainstormed and generated a list of possible themes to implement in the classroom. Taken into consideration are issues of appropriateness and relevance to the lives of the students. The instructional day has also been restructured to accommodate larger blocks of time. You understand the role of classroom environment and how to encourage your students to help you plan a meaningful curriculum by brainstorming a list of possibilities. With all of this in place, your next consideration might be how much integration should be a part of the instructional day. Do my students make connections in one area or throughout the day? Embarking on this question leads to discovering two common approaches towards integrated learning. Understanding the approaches provides valuable information.

> The teacher views him/herself as a reflective learner and researcher, reconsidering and expanding on avenues to learning.

The two common approaches to integrated curricula are intradisciplinary and interdisciplinary. An intradisciplinary approach is focused within an area, such as language arts or social science. An interdisciplinary approach goes beyond the single area and integrates across content areas. Each of these approaches offers students opportunities to make connections and links within and between ideas. In this chapter, the discussion will focus on an intradisciplinary approach to an integrated curriculum. The next chapter will highlight the interdisciplinary approach.

Intradisciplinary Teaching and Learning

An intradisciplinary approach to integrated learning is implemented in many classrooms throughout the country. The integration is found within a single discipline. Teachers and students come to understand connections and relationships among ideas, topics, skills, and concepts within the content area. The focus is on the explicit effort made to relate ideas, rather than to assume that students will automatically make their own connections (Fogarty, 1991). Through an intradisciplinary approach you and your students expand thinking patterns to make connections within the discipline.

One of the most common places to implement an intradisciplinary curriculum approach is in the discipline of language arts. Language arts encompasses reading, writing, and a wide variety of other tasks related to literacy. Integrating language arts is "an approach to learning, a way of thinking that respects the interrelationship of the language processes—reading, writing, speaking, and listening" (Routman, 1991, p. 276). These processes are intertwined and connected through many different pathways. They are tools utilized by learners to construct knowledge about the world, to make sense of the environment. Through language processes your students are able to organize and share experiences. As they engage in language-mediated activities, including reading, writing, speaking, and listening, they relate events to their own experiences to their own worlds (Britton, 1993). Language processes, thereby, are the organizing principles by which knowledge is shaped and represented.

With language processes as the focus of language arts integration, an intradisciplinary approach to teaching and learning highlights the connections between reading and writing events. Both are, in essence, a composing process, interpreting meaning through social acts of communication (Pearson, 1994). Your students participate in these activities using their background knowledge and prior experiences, creating understandings that are shared and negotiated among other students. In addition, they apply the knowledge discovered in reading to support writing and utilize writing knowledge to explore ideas and concepts in reading. Reading enables your learners to be exposed to the many different genres written for many different purposes. The importance of language conventions, such as spelling, punctuation, and usage, become apparent as students engage in writing. The potentialities of language are explored as learners create their own texts (Rosenblatt, 1994). On the other side, writing supports the reading process as learners construct their own texts by reading and reflecting on what they created. Reading comprehension is highlighted as your students construct cohesive texts about what they read. Through an intradisciplinary approach to language arts, your students are being asked to transverse the entire language and literacy landscape...not the single dimension of each (Pearson, 1994).

To facilitate the connections among language processes in language arts, you and your students decide on a focus theme. From there, a single narrative reflecting the theme, or a variety of books that examine the theme from multiple perspectives, is selected (Smith & Johnson, 1994). Literature becomes the core from which ideas and links are interpreted. Integrating reading, writing, listening, and speaking is quite easy when a piece of literature supports the activities.

Integrating reading, writing, listening, and speaking is quite easy when a piece of literature supports the activities.

An example of how an intradisciplinary language arts approach is conceived of in a classroom is presented below. Take note of the many ways in which the theme is addressed and then focused on throughout the thematic unit. Also think about the beginning steps discussed earlier and the roles they play in contributing to the success of the approach.

Intradisciplinary Theme Example

A third grade classroom has chosen the theme of ecology as their focus for language arts. The theme is important to the students in the classroom because the school has just initiated a recycling program in the cafeteria. There is quite a bit of interest in this new program, and students want to discover more information about the environment around them. The teacher has decided to use a variety of literature selections to support the theme. Books such as *One Day in the Tropical Rain Forest* (George, 1990), *Just a Dream* (Van Allsburg, 1990), *The Wump World* (Peet, 1970), and *Rain Forest Secrets* (Dorros, 1990) address a variety of ecological issues. The level of reading ability is taken into consideration, and students should have books available at different levels.

There are many possibilities in working with and discussing the books. With each book, there are activities to integrate the language processes. The teacher might have the students read the books in groups, forming literature groups. Literature groups encourage students to lead and participate in discussions. Topics for the discussions are selected by the students, based on interesting comments and passages found in the literature. They are able to choose their own avenue for discussions through literature groups, as well as have opportunities to share and collaborate. Meanings constructed in the text are shaped and reshaped by the participants of the literature circle. Students are actively engaged in the language processes of reading, speaking, and listening.

In an intradisciplinary approach to language arts, students engage in meaningful and purposeful literacy activities.

Students participate in many activities that support the reading/writing connection. Reading strategies and instruction are embedded within the context of reading and writing about the literature. Students are not working on decontextualized reading and writing tasks with no relevance to the literature or the world around. In an intradisciplinary approach to language arts, students engage in meaningful and purposeful literacy activities. Semantic maps/webs and reading logs are two such embedded strategies. Semantic maps/webs prove to be useful tools for organizing and integrating information in many different ways. In constructing these webs, students are encouraged to become active readers and utilize their background knowledge and experiences to make sense of the new texts (Heimlich & Pittelman, 1990). A sample semantic web used to organize information in *The Wump World* is provided on the following page.

A Semantic Web

Semantic webs highlight the relationships among the major events of a story. They help students focus on essential comprehension components. A sample semantic web for *The Wump World* is below. However, it is just an example and should not be considered the only correct response.

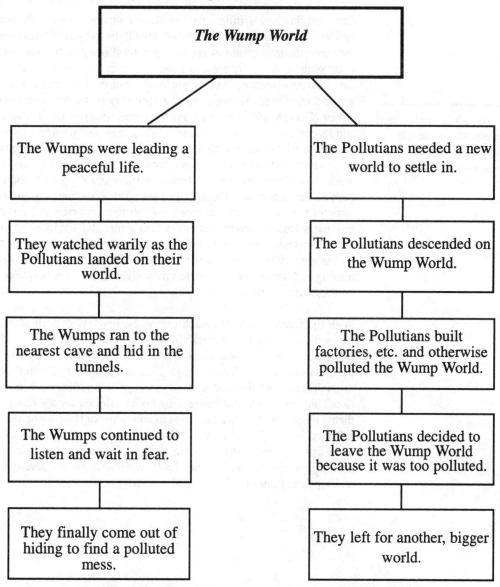

Reprinted from TCM 286, Thematic Unit: Ecology, *Teacher Created Materials, 1991*

Another reading strategy is the reading log which encourages students to record interesting or unfamiliar words and phrases. In small groups, students discuss the words/phrases and determine meanings from context clues and reference materials. These two strategies are examples of ways to address skills and instruction within the context of reading meaningful and relevant literature selections based on a chosen theme.

Other reading and writing activities include writing to city, state, and national officials and organizations about the recycling programs available, the importance of preserving natural areas for habitats, and other such ecologically minded issues. Letters to people outside of the classroom promote the real world application of integrated learning and teaching. Students reading *One Day in the Tropical Rain Forest* (George, 1990) might want to pursue issues of deforestation and its costs to the earth's creatures. They may also want to explore the format of journal writing as it is introduced in the book. Students can write about their own events occurring throughout the day or week. This format enables students to explore other types of writing beyond the narrative. Through journal writing students develop a sense of their own voices and feelings. Writing underscores ways to link ideas from different sections within a text and across different books students are exposed to in literature circles (Raphael & McMahon, 1994). The connections and interrelationship between reading and writing processes are emphasized in an intradisciplinary language arts curriculum.

> Through journal writing students develop a sense of their own voice and feelings.

With the focus of this approach on the explicitness of formulating connections in and out of texts and ideas, students should be provided with activities to practice linking ideas together within a single text or various texts. The form on page 33 is an opportunity for students to think about and respond to ideas presented across literature selections. For example, students reading books selected for the ecology theme might identify an issue, such as solutions for the environment, reflected by the different books. From this activity students are able to identify connections they value and find important to the understandings of the unit and theme. Explicit connections are developed and supported through the use of this activity.

Connecting Ideas Among Texts

Name _____

Date _____

Title_____

Title _____

Title _____

Throughout the ecology unit, teachers and students are engaged in making connections between and among ideas, skills, and concepts. Ideas presented in one context often appear in other contexts. Known as intertextuality, students generate connections and links among different texts (Hartman, 1994). As connections are established, learners construct a web of meanings. Meanings constantly evolve as students discover new texts and new insights. "The understandings in one text or passage 'spill over' into understandings of other texts—both past and future" (Hartman, 1994, p. 623). Students engaged in an intradisciplinary approach to language arts encounter intertextuality frequently. Reading and discussing different books with a common theme, writing for different purposes, and engaging in speaking and listening activities promote intertextual relationships between and among the various ideas within the discipline. As students engage in and participate in the intradisciplinary approach, they come to understand the integrative nature of learning and that the language processes of reading, writing, speaking, and listening are intertwined and interconnected in many ways.

> Students engaged in an intradisciplinary approach to language arts encounter intertextuality frequently.

Intradisciplinary Content Areas

The focus of this chapter up to now has been on the language arts component of the curriculum. While the intradisciplinary approach to language arts is the most popular, it is important to consider the other content areas. Social studies, science, and mathematics also lend themselves to an integrated intradisciplinary approach. There are many concepts and processes learners encounter in each discipline. Creating explicit connections among processes and ideas within a single discipline is possible, given the nature of an intradisciplinary approach. Social studies, for example, has under its umbrella community issues, people and places, geography, government, history, and geography. Scientific thinking involves many processes, including questioning, hypothesizing, gathering data, drawing conclusions, analyzing, and reporting. Mathematical concepts and problem-solving strategies are connected in many ways. Within the various disciplines there are opportunities to make connections between and among ideas, skills, and concepts. An intradisciplinary approach to the content areas enables students and teachers to develop understandings beyond the surface level.

Social studies with its many areas of study is a discipline that can easily adopt an intradisciplinary approach. Naturally, the areas are interrelated and have connections that are apparent from the outset. Through an intradisciplinary approach, the road to connections becomes more intricate and complex. Students learn to view social studies not as a series of isolated facts and concepts, but rather as a whole, with each area influencing and shaping the others. An example is the theme exploring the unknown. Learning about explorers discovering new areas of the world can be connected to understanding map making skills and concepts. Students may create maps of their own neighborhoods, applying newly acquired information to real world experiences. They may also create maps of uncharted territory, such as space. What information do they already know? What information do they wish they knew? What supplies are necessary? Who is going with them? This activity will provide students with a sense of what earlier explorers faced when they ventured off to new lands. The theme of exploring the unknown can be expanded to discussing personal fears of students as they experience events in the world and solutions they have to conquering those fears. As you can see, there are many ways to create connections and associations between ideas and concepts. Encouraging connections of this nature, along with the numerous others students will generate, supports the notion that an intradisciplinary approach to social studies helps students make connections between actions and results in a society.

Science and mathematics are two other disciplines that can be taught through an intradisciplinary approach. Process skills are integrated to foster connections. Scientific thinking focuses on the relationships among process skills. The steps involved in scientific thinking are interrelated and connected. For example, some students may have observed a piece of wood floating in a puddle on the playground after a recent rainstorm. This observation can lead to hypotheses about which items float and which do not. Experiments are then conducted on various materials and whether they float. Data is collected and results are analyzed, leading to conclusions. These conclusions are related to the original observation. As students participate in experiments, they are utilizing and integrating process skills. Approaching science through experiments supports the integration of processing skills.

Mathematical thinking is very similar. Discovering connections and relationships among mathematical processes enables students to view mathematics as a whole, rather than bits and pieces of information. Patterning, for instance, is a connecting thread in math curriculum. Young students create patterns with objects and colors. Older students try to discover patterns in numbers and algorithms. Addressing patterns throughout the math curriculum exemplifies the integrative nature of mathematical thinking. As students make connections within the processing skills, the science and math curriculum is enhanced.

Science and mathematics are two other disciplines that can be taught through an intradisciplinary approach.

Concluding Remarks

An intradisciplinary approach to the curriculum is one way to integrate ideas and concepts. The integration is within a single discipline. The focus for the intradisciplinary approach is on the explicit connections made in a specific content area. The most common discipline to utilize an intradisciplinary approach is language arts. The language processes of reading, writing, speaking, and listening are interrelated and intertwined in many ways. Students engage in many activities that support connections among and between the language processes. In an intradisciplinary approach to the language arts, a theme is the unifying component. Students participate in reading and writing activities based on the theme, either in one piece of literature or in a variety of literature selections. The connections students construct are based on the idea of intertextuality, whereby information and knowledge gathered from one text will often appear in another context. Learners link the information in many and diverse ways, depending on their prior background knowledge and experiences. In addition to the language arts, the other disciplines of social studies, science, and mathematics can also be approached through an intradisciplinary format. Each of these content areas has numerous ideas, skills, and concepts that can be linked and connected. The intradisciplinary approach to an integrated curriculum is beneficial to you and your students alike. Discovering connections and making them explicit encourages your students to think about the integrative nature of events in and out of the classroom.

> The focus for the intradisciplinary approach is on the explicit connections made in a specific content area.

Interdisciplinary Curriculum

What Makes This Approach Different?

An interdisciplinary approach to the curriculum includes all of the content areas under one unifying theme. "This approach is a comprehensive learning experience that combines skills and questions from more than one discipline to examine a central theme, issue, situation, inquiry, or topic" (Smith & Johnson, 1994, p. 200). An interdisciplinary approach views disciplines in a fashion similar to that of the real world. Novelists, mathematicians, scientists, historians, and others come together to understand events in the world. Each brings his/her own expertise to the event, shaping and negotiating the understandings that emerge.

> An interdisciplinary approach to the curriculum includes all of the content areas under one unifying theme.

The interdisciplinary approach to the curriculum encourages students to come into activities and tasks, utilizing their background knowledge to construct meanings. Through these understandings learners make connections. They have the opportunity to consider the way in which knowledge converges and changes with each connection. Connections are shaped and reshaped as learners interpret meanings and negotiate understandings.

An interdisciplinary approach to the curriculum begins as does the intradisciplinary one. You and your students have brainstormed a list of possible themes to study, the classroom environment is supportive of integrated learning, and the instructional day has been restructured to accommodate the larger blocks of time necessary to participate in projects. The primary difference between the two approaches is in the amount of integration among ideas and concepts. An interdisciplinary approach to the curriculum encourages teachers and students to integrate ideas and concepts through many different pathways. It is an all-consuming approach to learning and teaching. As students and teachers participate in discovering the multitude of connections and associations, it is important to organize and plan the various activities and projects. Utilizing curriculum webs, such as those discussed earlier, will aid the organization. As you write in activities and projects, you may want to highlight the specific skills and concepts being taught. When you view the overall web, the skills will stand out and you will quickly notice if any are missing. This organization is to help insure that the necessary skills and concepts are being adequately addressed within the context of the theme.

> The classroom becomes a museum, publishing house, art studio, theater, computer center, court, congress, science lab, and library.

Interdisciplinary Teaching and Learning

An interdisciplinary approach to the curriculum enables learners to gather knowledge holistically, rather than in compartmentalized pieces. Throughout the instructional day the focus is on a unifying theme, whether students are engaged in a reading or writing activity or in a science activity. The classroom becomes a museum, publishing house, art studio, theater, computer center, court, congress, science lab, and library. As your students explore a theme, undiscovered connections and associations may emerge, providing your students with deeper understandings of the theme and its relationship to the world.

With all content areas involved in an interdisciplinary approach to learning, there is not one discipline that fares better or is integrated more than the others. Integration occurs throughout the disciplines. However, it is critical to the success of an intradisciplinary approach that the integration of ideas and skills is authentic and relevant, not just to satisfy the cutting across discipline lines. "Effective curriculum integration occurs when the content from one subject area is used to enhance or enrich the content of another" (Lapp & Flood, 1994, p. 418).

Activities developed in an interdisciplinary approach reinforce the interrelationship among ideas and concepts. These activities tie the theme and the content together in an authentic learning environment.

As your students become engaged in the activities and create connections, it is possible to gain insight into their thinking and learning patterns. "It is through what children actually conceive, organize, do and present to us and others that their intellectual functioning can be seen and understood most clearly" (Stevenson & Carr, 1993, p. 21). Activities in an interdisciplinary approach to the curriculum give students the opportunity to demonstrate the pathways and avenues they used to build meaning.

Integration of literacy tasks into areas such as math and science are making inroads into the process of integration. Providing students with opportunities to read and write about mathematical and scientific concepts enables them to construct connections between the disciplines. It is through the literacy process that math and science content is taught and developed. Acquiring information, understanding procedures, solving problems, and conducting experiments requires the application of a variety of literacy skills (Casteel & Isom, 1994). Math problems often are approached through reading and writing activities. Students are now keeping math journals where problems are solved and written descriptions are included on how the process was completed.

> Integration of literacy tasks into areas such as math and science are making inroads into the process of integration.

Comparing literacy and science process skills, it is possible to view the connections and similarities between them. With literacy tasks, students identify the purpose and predict the outcome. In science, students make an observation and hypothesize why it may be so. Continuing on with similarities, literacy tasks involve organizing ideas, composing thoughts, and evaluating/revising ideas. Science tasks include gathering data, drawing conclusions, and analyzing results. Both disciplines have some form of communication at the end of the tasks, whether it is reporting the results or publishing the piece of work. While the processes are not identical, they do overlap in important ways. Writing fosters the acquisition of process skills in math and science. Through writing activities, students utilize their prior knowledge, organize information, and become more involved in learning mathematical and scientific knowledge. Merging literacy with math and science is a way of creating connections and pathways among the disciplines.

An interdisciplinary approach to the curriculum highlights the connections students create as your students explore a theme. Similar to the last chapter, examples of interdisciplinary approaches to the curriculum are discussed. One is an upper grade unit, the other primary. Again, observe how the theme is the central focus for learning.

An Upper Grade Interdisciplinary Unit Example

In this example, fifth grade students have selected to study the theme the United States constitution. This theme is in accordance with many state and district frameworks throughout the country. The theme is of particular interest to these students because of the recent uprisings throughout the world, heard of nightly on the news. Students in this class are wondering what makes the United States different in their beliefs and where these beliefs generated. The teacher is sensitive to the interests of the students and suggests that they may want to explore the United States Constitution. Many students are interested in knowing more about the U. S. Constitution because they had created their own classroom constitution, outlining appropriate classroom behavior and goals for the year. The theme, then, holds the interest of the students and lends itself to many activities that will support skills in the often mandated curriculum.

Literature selections often become the primary reading selections and are used throughout the unit.

After selecting the theme, the teacher and students locate narratives and literature that develop and expand the chosen theme. Literature selections often become the primary reading selections and are used throughout the unit. It is important, then, to spend some time gathering books that are interesting and motivating for the students. Book titles included for this theme are *Shh! We're Writing the Constitution* (Fritz, 1987), *We the People: The Constitution of the United States of America* (Spier, 1987), *If You Were There When They Signed the Constitution* (Levy, 1987), *Ben and Me* (Lawson, 1988), and biographies about such influential people as Alexander Hamilton, Thomas Jefferson, and James Madison. The literature selections should be broad enough to meet the developmental needs and abilities of all students in the classroom. Utilizing the range of literature from picture books to chapter books and historical fiction to nonfiction will enable students to successfully participate on many levels. Sometimes locating literature selections to appropriately address the theme directly is difficult to find. When this occurs, the teacher may want to slightly alter the theme to fit the literature that can be found.

The next critical step in the process is to identify learning outcomes and objectives students will be exposed to throughout the course of the thematic unit. Learning outcomes are what the students are going to experience and learn. In this thematic unit, students will learn about the role and importance of the United States Constitution as it relates to the formation of our government and as it impacts the daily lives of the students. Students will experience working together in groups to effectively solve problems, use literacy skills to think and communicate, and gain a greater understanding of how learning patterns and connections are constructed. From the learning outcomes, objectives are developed that highlight the processes the students encounter as they participate in the thematic unit (Smith & Johnson, 1994). An important objective in an interdisciplinary approach to the curriculum is "connecting all of the content areas that permit transference of information so students can see and build relationships among all disciplines" (Smith & Johnson, 1994, p. 205). Identifying learning outcomes and objectives provides teachers and students with a focus as they immerse themselves in the theme.

Activities and projects are developed from the learning outcomes and objectives. This is where integration between and among disciplines becomes apparent. Activities and projects incorporate skills and concepts from the different disciplines to create meaningful and relevant learning opportunities. Students working with the theme of the U.S. Constitution participate in a wide variety of tasks. The tasks range from whole group discussions, to smaller group problem solving projects, to individual writing assignments. As students explore and expand upon the content and knowledge, new connections and thinking patterns emerge. Embedded within the connections are skills and concepts necessary to participate in the real world.

Activities and projects incorporate skills and concepts from the different disciplines to create meaningful and relevant learning opportunities.

Developing the activities and projects often involves locating and utilizing resources beyond the selected texts. The teacher and students actively participate in gathering the materials and resources necessary. Resources may include guest speakers from the community, field trips, films, information and brochures from museums and historical places, and a host of other materials to successfully implement and teach the thematic unit.

Once the activities and projects have been developed to teach the skills and concepts, the next step is to establish the evaluation criteria. It is important to identify the practices and strategies of evaluation before the unit begins to ensure that students are assessed on the content and information developed in the thematic unit. Identifying assessment practices also helps teachers and students see if objectives and outcomes are correlated. A more complete and detailed discussion of evaluation and assessment is provided in the upcoming chapter.

Samples of the ways in which the students and teacher have chosen to integrate the curriculum are available on the following pages. Ideas for language arts, mathematics, social studies, science, art, and music are included. The samples are specific to the theme of the U.S. Constitution. The purpose of the examples is to provide activities that demonstrate the integrated nature of a thematic unit.

Selecting ideas from a variety of resources, the activities are interesting and motivating to students, while at the same time addressing critical skills and concepts. The examples are meant to provide you with a frame of reference on how a thematic unit might be conceived in the classroom. Many of the activities are applicable to other thematic units. The activities and projects are identified by the content area for easy reference. As these activities are applied in the classroom, the division between content areas becomes less apparent. It is important to remember that an integrated approach to the curriculum is flexible and dynamic. Learners will build their own connections from the activities and projects. The success of an interdisciplinary approach is to recognize flexibility and encourage students to travel on different avenues, creating new interpretations of the information.

Many of the literature selections within this thematic unit focus on the chronology of historical events.

Language Arts. Beginning with the literature selections and language arts, students are engaged in reading and responding to the various texts chosen to complement the theme of the U.S. Constitution. Grouped according to their interests, the students participate in literature groups. The topics for discussions are generated by the students themselves, reflecting their interests and concerns. As part of the literature group, students are asked to record any words or phrases that caught their attention or that they do not understand. In the discussion, words and phrases can be addressed, providing students with an authentic and relevant purpose for seeking new information. Encouraging students to develop vocabulary through the context of the literature ensures authenticity for the task.

Many of the literature selections within this thematic unit focus on the chronology of historical events. *Shh! We're Writing the Constitution* (Fritz, 1987) discusses the proceedings of the historic meetings where the Constitution was written. The biographies about the various influential people are generally written in chronological order, identifying significant periods and events in their lives. *If You Were There When They Signed the Constitution* (Levy, 1987) also describes the events of the times, along with a look at the daily lives of those living in that time period. Given the tendency of these selections to organize their information in a chronological format, an activity that lends itself to making connections between authors and students is a journal or diary. Students can either write about their own lives as similar or different to those in an earlier time or imagine the lives of characters and people within their literature selections. Journal writing enables students to write about ideas and topics that are of interest to them. The focus is not on the mechanics of writing, but rather the freedom of expression. Students should be encouraged to expand and explore the conventions of language through their journal writing, developing ways to clearly express their feelings and beliefs.

Providing opportunities for learners to write in formats similar to what they are reading enhances connections made between reading and writing events.

Fostering the connection between real world and classroom activities is an important aspect of interdisciplinary learning and teaching. The daily newspaper is an excellent resource that promotes this connection. Within the theme of the U.S. Constitution students can utilize the newspaper to locate current happenings related to the Constitution and the Bill of Rights. Helping students make connections between events of the past and current events is critical to developing students' sense of the role historical events play in their own lives. The more opportunities teachers and students have to integrate and connect ideas and concepts learned in the classroom to the outside world, the more successful and purposeful the learning and thinking become.

An additional activity designed to promote literacy skills is to construct a hornbook, quill, and parchment representing literacy materials of the time period. If possible, bringing in examples of these materials, or pictures of them, will help students visualize how the materials were used. See page 45 for directions on making these materials. While this page is specific to making these materials, the intention is to provide ideas on how projects related to the theme can be implemented in the classroom with relative ease. There are numerous activities that can be implemented using the hornbook, quill, and parchment. Students can recreate the classroom setting of the time period by writing their lessons on the parchment with the quill and by teaching younger students the alphabet and numbers with the hornbook. Students may even want to research the origins of these materials. These activities support reading and writing connections to construct meaning about the time period as it relates to the theme of the U.S. Constitution.

Throughout the language arts activities, students are addressing skills and concepts identified in the state and district framework, as well as in teachers' editions of textbooks and other resources. Within these examples of activities, students are becoming familiar with new vocabulary words, identifying cause and effect, comparing and contrasting events in the literature selections, identifying main and supporting ideas, and are being exposed to different genres. The variety of genres encourages students to view written texts for various purposes. They are able to write in many formats, encouraging a perspective that writing serves many purposes. Students are also reading literature selections for information and for pleasure. This helps to support motivation and interest in reading and writing

> Fostering the connection between real world and classroom activities is an important aspect of interdisciplinary learning and teaching.

events. These skills are only a few of the highlighted ones on the curriculum web that are addressed through activities in the U. S. Constitution theme.

The described language arts activities are examples of the many possibilities available to learners and teachers engaged in an interdisciplinary approach to thinking and learning. Throughout the theme study unit on the U. S. Constitution, students are active participants in constructing their own meaningful connections. For instance, a student may develop a thorough understanding of how biographies are constructed from reading many literature selections in the genre. The student is knowledgeable on what type of information is included, in what ways the events in the text are organized, and the historical importance of the person being read about. Another student also engaged in the U. S. Constitution theme might delve into something completely different. This student may have developed a strong interest in reading current news articles for evidence of how the Constitution influences our daily lives. As she/he reads the daily newspaper, the structure of news articles catches this learner's eyes and he/she is inspired to write an article for the school newspaper. These two examples provide an understanding that the students will take away from the theme unit ideas and concepts that are of particular interest to them. It is important as the teacher to encourage flexibility as learners gather different pieces of knowledge to construct their own learning.

Re-creating Constitutional Times

The year 1787 is so long ago that it may be difficult to imagining what living conditions might have been like then. Students were taught in one-room school houses. Lessons were written with a quill on parchment, and the alphabet was learned with the help of a hornbook.

Hornbooks

Materials: a template pattern of a hornbook, scissors, glue, cardboard (from a cereal box), black marking pen

Directions:
- Make copies of the pattern. Give each student one.
- Have students cut out the hornbook and glue to a piece of cardboard; let dry.
- Students then cut the cardboard to the shape of the hornbook. With a black marking pen, have them write the letters of the alphabet and numerals.

Quills

Materials: wing feather from a turkey, crow, seagull, or goose; sharp knife; pencil; liquid ink

Directions:
- With the knife make an angled cut on the underside of the wing tip.
- Cut the tip square.
- Slit the tip just a little and press open with a pencil.

Parchment

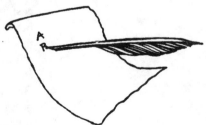

Materials: brown paper shopping bags, scissors

Directions:
- With the scissors, cut open the brown paper bags.
- To make sheets with ragged edges, tear by hand.
- With a quill and ink, write lessons onto the "parchment."

Reprinted from TCM 582 Thematic Unit: U. S. Constitution, *Teacher Created Materials, 1993*

<u>Mathematics</u>. Moving through the disciplines, math activities in an interdisciplinary approach should resemble math practiced in and out of the classroom. In many instances, problematic situations are the basis for math outside the classroom. Math is frequently embedded in the day-to-day routine, from shopping and banking to estimating distances and playing games. As students confront math-oriented problems outside the classroom, they utilize a variety of skills and concepts from different disciplines, such as social studies and literacy. They read, write, and share their thinking patterns as they solve problems. Math tasks inside the classroom should be approached in a similar fashion, implementing a variety of skills and concepts. Encouraging students to view math as a socially interactive process where the focus is to create and share mathematical thinking and as a tool for making sense of the world gives rise to the authenticity of math in the classroom. As teachers empower students to develop their own thinking patterns and understandings in mathematical concepts, "...students work together to make sense of mathematics; rely more on themselves to determine whether something is mathematically correct; learn to reason mathematically; learn to conjecture, invent, and solve problems; and connect mathematical ideas and applications" (Winograd & Higgins, 1994, p. 313–314).

In an interdisciplinary approach to the curriculum, the math problems students formulate are related to the theme being studied.

Writing, solving, and sharing their own math problems enables students to become engaged in authentic uses of mathematics. When students are able to generate and create story problems, their own experiences and connections become salient to the problems. Teachers are able to gain insights into the students' thinking patterns and understandings related to mathematical issues. In an interdisciplinary approach to the curriculum, the math problems students formulate are related to the theme being studied. In the example thematic unit, U. S. Constitution, students may write story problems comparing and contrasting the cost of living in the late 1700's and the cost of living today. Problems involving the traveled distances between the capital cities and Philadelphia for the delegates' meeting might be generated. Students may even create a graph to display the information. It is important to remember that the math activities should remain authentic and purposeful to the learning. Recalling Brophy and Alleman (1991), "cutting across subject lines" does not necessarily promote integrated learning. Students' roles as "problem-finders and problem-solvers, of readers and writers, of listeners and talkers, and of critics and collaborators" enables them to construct pathways of understandings and connections (Winograd & Higgins, 1994, p. 316).

The math skills in the sample activities are graphing, comparison, and algorithms involving addition, subtraction, multiplication, division, ratios and percentages. Embedding the skills within the activities and the theme creates an atmosphere that math is not abstract and irrelevant to their lives, but is necessary and applicable to real world situations.

Social Studies. Integration of ideas in this discipline is throughout the thematic unit. Students participate in many activities that lend themselves to a historical and a geographical perspective. Activities include developing a time line to correspond with events in one of the literature selections, researching and reporting on historical key figures, comparing gender roles of the late 1700's to today, studying and mapping the area from which the delegates traveled, and developing understandings of the role of the Constitution in our history and in the present day. Through these activities and many others similar in nature, students are able to integrate the different disciplines into the ideas and concepts from the state or district framework.

> Students have the opportunity to develop knowledge in concrete and meaningful ways.

Literacy tasks play a large role in social studies as students read, write, speak, and listen for many purposes. Students may take an active role in writing letters to government officials concerning a matter of importance or rights. They may also set up a mock Congress or court to enact the process of a bill being passed or how laws are enforced. Through these activities, oral language and listening skills are reinforced. Students may also participate in amending and ratifying their own classroom constitution now that they have new knowledge about the U. S. Constitution and the role it plays in our society. These activities are meaningful and relevant to the lives of the students as they become active citizens in the country. Developing an understanding of the government and its functions provides students with the opportunity to initiate changes and make decisions regarding the future state of our nation.

Addressing such skills and concepts as understanding time and historical relevance, becoming familiar with historical figures of the country, understanding the democratic system of our government, and developing an understanding of citizenship are implied throughout the activities in the unit. Students have the opportunity to develop knowledge in concrete and meaningful ways.

Science. With regard to science, activities and projects related to the theme are developed. Students are actively reading about Benjamin Franklin, one of the key historical figures of the time period. In addition to his role as statesman, he was also an inventor and scientist. In the book *Ben and Me* (Lawson, 1988), Franklin's inventions and experiments are discussed. From reading about Franklin's experiments in electricity, students may be motivated to conduct their own experiments on the properties of electricity. On the following page are some ideas for possible experiments for the classroom.

Scientific thinking and processing skills are developed and connected to the theme through a variety of ways. Students may also be interested in researching some of the other inventions of the time period, such as hot air balloons, bifocals, the seismograph, and the steam engine. Additionally, the discovery of the planet, Uranus, occurred. Projects involving the planets and visiting a planetarium may be included. As you can see with this suggestion, the theme U. S. Constitution can be expanded to include alternative projects not commonly thought of as fitting in. Important to remember is that the students are interested and that the connection makes sense to them.

Scientific thinking and processing skills are developed and connected to the theme through a variety of ways.

Art/Music/Drama. Art, music, and drama projects are interwoven throughout the thematic unit. Students discuss and recreate fashionable clothing of the period, sing period songs, and observe the artwork of the late 1700's. They may draw and paint portraits of friends and family that demonstrate a technique and style similar to those frequently done of historical figures.

Students enjoy any opportunity for drama. They might want to take on roles of famous statesman and colonists and enact some of the historical meetings held to write the Constitution. They could also engage in interviewing and reporting on the events of the time period. Drama encourages students to gain perspective on character motivation and to have better understandings of why events happened the way they did.

Electrifying Experiences

Benjamin Franklin was a man of many talents. He was a statesman, writer, inventor, and a scientist, among other things. One of his most memorable experiments involved a kite, a key, and a storm cloud. In order to investigate the changes in storm clouds, Franklin flew a kite into a billowing storm cloud. He had tied a key to the end of the kite line. When the electrical charge ran down the wet kite line it finally hit the key where sparks flashed. It is a wonder that Franklin was not killed or injured! Learn about some of the properties of electricity with the following projects.

Static Electricity Chamber

In a storm cloud static electricity is formed when tiny water droplets and ice particles rub together. This results in lightning. Another kind of static electricity can occur when clothes rub together. When have you experienced static electricity? What did it feel like?

Materials: colored art tissue, scissors, box with plastic lid (such as a stationery box)

Procedure: Supply each group with the materials listed above. Challenge them to use those materials to demonstrate static electricity in action.

Solution: Cut the tissue into squares or any small shape. Place six or eight of them into the box and cover with the lid. Rub a hand across the lid. Watch as the tissue shapes rise to the surface of the lid.

Predicting Static

Materials: paper, wood, rubber, plastic, and glass objects (such as foam, paper, and plastic cups; glass jars; large craft sticks; an eraser; plastic comb); wool cloth; torn bits of tissue paper; paper and pencil

Procedure: Divide into pairs or small groups. Each group receives the paper, wood, rubber, plastic, and glass objects.

- Before beginning the experiment, predict which materials will create static electricity. Record your guess and expectations on a sheet of paper. Circle those that make the best static electricity.
- Test your hypotheses. Rub each material with the wool cloth and then hold it above the bits of tissue to test whether the materials are attracted or not.
- Discuss the results in a whole group.

Static Demonstration

Materials: plastic comb, wool cloth, slow running tap water

Procedure:

- Before beginning the experiment, what do you think will happen when water is added to the experiment of static electricity? Record your hypotheses on a sheet of paper.
- Rub the comb with the cloth. Hold the charged comb next to the running water.
- Record what happens. Why do you think this is so?
- Discuss results with the group.

Reprinted from TCM 582 Thematic Unit: U. S. Constitution, *Teacher Created Materials, 1993*

As you may have noticed in this thematic unit example, the theme has many branches and possibilities. From the mock courthouse and gathering information on travel distances to electricity and the planets, many activities are included under one theme. As students participate in the activities and construct their own pathways of learning, the connections will be complex and diverse. What is critical is that the students should be able to justify their own specific pathways to learning and knowledge. One of the exciting aspects of an interdisciplinary approach to the curriculum is this element of diversity and surprise. In a flexible and dynamic curriculum, learning happens in many different and complex ways.

An interdisciplinary approach to the curriculum has enabled this fifth grade classroom to construct meaning in diverse and complex ways. Students have become knowledgeable about the U. S. Constitution its relationship to their own lives, studied historical figures of the time period, created artifacts from the late 1700's, studied and experimented with electricity, participated in a mock Congress and courthouse, and developed a deeper understanding of the ways in which connections can be constructed. Throughout the unit, students utilized their own prior knowledge and experiences to make sense of the new information. They worked in groups and collaborated on many activities. Students participated in meaningful and purposeful activities, integrating knowledge between and among disciplines and environments.

A Primary Interdisciplinary Unit Example

In this example, a first grade is studying the ocean and sea life. The students do not live near the ocean, but have many references to sea life in their lives. Many of the students have seen movies such as *Free Willy* and *The Little Mermaid*. A local sports team is named "Sharks." During the brainstorming session, a popular topic mentioned was sharks. Some students also mentioned whales and seals. They are interested in knowing more about these animals and where they live. A couple of students expressed an interest in talking about the fish they have at home as pets. The teacher is aware that if she/he hooks into the interests of the students, they will be more motivated to learn. An important point here is to be open to possible themes arising from unique, often not academic, places. Although these students may not have the opportunity to experience the ocean firsthand, they are highly motivated and interested in the topic. After some discussion, a theme of sea life is decided upon.

Just as in the upper grade unit, the teacher uses frameworks and other resources to identify skills and concepts appropriate for the first

One of the exciting aspects of an interdisciplinary approach to the curriculum is this element of diversity and surprise.

grade. Students will be exposed to skills such as emergent literacy strategies, writing, numeration, patterning, graphing, comparing/contrasting, predicting, and learning about their families and homes. These skills are embedded within the activities and projects. There will be opportunities for students to develop and refine their oral language skills as they participate in cooperative groups and discussions. Students will also be engaged in critical thinking as they explore the theme of sea life.

Within the theme are many choices of literature selections. The genres range from nonfiction and informational to fiction. Students are exposed to the different genres to increase their awareness of the many types of books available and of the existence of factual information in many stories and literature selections. In this unit, the selections include *Swimmy* (Lionni, 1963), *The Whale's Song* (Sheldon, 1991), *I Am the Ocean* (Marshak, 1991), *A House for Hermit Crab* (Carle, 1987), *Oceans*, (Whitfield, 1991), and *Animals of Sea and Shore* (Podendorf, 1982). All of these choices encourage young students to learn more about sea life, the ocean, and how this knowledge will impact and influence their own lives. Connections between the students' lives and the theme are often initiated through the various literature selections.

> Language arts in the primary grades involves many activities and projects addressing emergent literacy skills and strategies.

Language Arts. Language arts in the primary grades involves many activities and projects addressing emergent literacy skills and strategies. Young students are beginning to engage in reading and writing events. They listen to and discuss stories about the sea, learn new vocabulary words, recognize alphabet letters through games and projects, participate in activities encouraging letter/sound correspondence, and write their own stories.

By reading the story *A House for Hermit Crab* (Carle, 1987), the teacher encourages students to develop vocabulary for the different animals Hermit Crab invites to live on his shell. Animals such as sea anemones, starfish, snails, sea urchins, and lanternfish are included in the story. Additionally, this story introduces the months of the year as Hermit Crab travels through the ocean, adding to his shell. Vocabulary for the months of the year can also be included in learning sight words for reading.

Students may incorporate the format of this story into their own writing. They may create a book that has each month of the year on a separate page. As the young writer moves through the book, ideas and objects are added to the original concept. For example, the student may want to have himself/herself as the main character and add things as the story progresses.

Other literature selections, such as *Animals of Sea and Shore* (Podendorf, 1982) and *Oceans* (Whitfield, 1991) are good resources for students to learn factual information. Young readers may choose to write factual statements about the ocean that can then be made into a class book. Each student can contribute to the book, creating a group project for the class library. It also enables the teacher to observe the level of knowledge and development each student has in literacy skills. Students are able to utilize their own background knowledge and experiences to construct meaningful and relevant ideas for the book. Reflecting on the original brainstorming session, some may even come to learn about the strength of sharks and why a sports team would want to be named Sharks. Throughout this activity and others, the teacher also provides opportunities to observe the connections students make between reading and writing activities and ideas presented through the theme of sea life.

Social Studies. For many primary grades, the social studies curriculum consists of learning about yourself and your family. As students learn about these concepts, they can begin to apply them to other living creatures. Learning about sea animals and how they are similar to and different from humans can be a powerful connection for some students. Students may wonder about baby animals and how they grow. Do all mothers teach their babies, or do some fathers become involved in the teaching? Students learn about the different family structures for different animals.

Another activity in the realm of social studies would be to observe and discuss how the character in Leo Lionni's *Swimmy* feels because he is different from the rest of the fish. Discussions involving differences among people, tolerance, and acceptance could be part of the ongoing theme.

In many different ways, students come to view themselves and their families through expanded lenses. They are able to discuss similarities and differences about the animal kingdom with their peers. Integrating activities into the sea life theme encourages students to construct their own pathways for learning and exploring the world.

Mathematics. The students in this first grade are actively engaged in exploring and discovering patterns. The activities supporting the math curriculum utilize objects from the ocean, such as sea shells, pebbles, and sand. Students can hide the shells in the sand and go on a shell hunt for a predetermined number. They can classify and sort the shells according to attributes. Students can also graph the number of types of shells and pebbles they have. An activity involving graphing is included on page 54.

> Learning about sea animals and how they are similar to and different from humans can be a powerful connection for some students.

Students are in the emergent stages of writing and should be encouraged to draw and write math story problems. These problems can relate to the theme of sea life by having students incorporate types of fish and sea life into the problem. These problems may include the skills of addition and subtraction. A real world application is to gather prices on salt water fish from the local pet store and do some math problems involving money. Some students may not be ready for the more abstract concepts with money, but the activity can be adapted to the developmental level of the students.

Mathematical skills and concepts are integrated throughout these activities. Manipulatives and hands-on experiences are provided to develop the concreteness necessary as young students explore math and begin to make sense of it.

Living Graphs

Do this as a group activity so that all the children participate in making and then interpreting the graph.

"What Is Your Favorite Sea Animal?" Graph

Preparation: Make a graph on chart paper as shown in the diagram below. Copy several pictures of sea animals. Make the columns in the graph wide enough to fit the pictures.

Making the Graph: Work with a small group of children at a time. Ask each child to tell you his/her favorite sea animal from the choices available and to choose it from the pile. Print or have the children print their names on their choices. Then help each child paste the card in the correct place on the graph. When everyone has had a turn, call the children together to interpret the graph.

Interpreting the Graph:

• Ask several children to show where they pasted their squares.

• Ask all children who liked crabs best to raise their hands.

• Ask all children who liked eels best to stand up and turn around.

• Ask all children who liked jellyfish best to jump up and down. Count the children who liked jellyfish best. Then count the jellyfish cards on the graph. Compare and discuss. Do the same for each sea animal.

• Ask which sea animal is the most popular. How do they know?

• Ask which sea animal is least popular. How do they know?

• Display the graph in the classroom.

Helena		
Felipe		Sue
Rick	Marie	Mike
crab	eel	jellyfish

Reprinted from TCM 254 Thematic Unit: Sea Animals, *Teacher Created Materials, 1993*

<u>Science</u>. The theme of sea life is one that is easily integrated into science. Many activities and projects are based on scientific thinking. Students can observe the similarities and differences in the different types of sea life. Why do whales have blow holes and other animals do not? Students can learn about the different parts of mollusks and other sea animals. As students read and study about the animals, they may also learn about why these animals do not live in the pond or lake. Discovering the properties of salt water is an activity that is best approached through experiments. Students can observe, hypothesize, gather data, record data, analyze, and draw conclusions about salt water and fresh water. On page 57 is an example of how to set up salt water experiments in the classroom. Encouraging students to write and draw their conclusions promotes the integration of literacy tasks in science.

Students engaged in science activities are developing their skills in scientific thinking and processing. They are exploring the reasons why animals have certain attributes and characteristics. Students may also develop understandings of how animals and plants survive under water when humans cannot. Connecting the newly acquired information to students' own lives makes the learning process more meaningful and relevant.

<u>Art/Music/Drama</u>. The disciplines of art, music, and drama are frequently part of the instructional day in the primary grades. Students often engage in drawing and singing as they learn new ideas and concepts. Within the discipline, there are skills that can be addressed through the theme of sea life. Students can explore colors and how to mix and blend them. This skill fits nicely into a project where students paint fish and print them on large sheets of paper. In painting the fish, students can create and blend colors. Other activities include painting murals of the different animals and plants in the ocean, using shells and other objects for sea companions, and making sponge prints of different animals.

The style of art in both *Swimmy* (Lionni, 1963) and *A House for Hermit Crab* (Carle, 1987) is interesting for students to replicate. Students can experiment with watercolors and sponges to create similar effects in their own pictures of the sea.

For music and drama, students can sing songs about the ocean and role-play different animals in the ocean. Creating puppets of sea animals encourages young students to participate in oral language activities.

The disciplines of art, music, and drama are frequently part of the instructional day in the primary grades.

As you can see, the interdisciplinary nature of the theme of sea life is easily implemented in the classroom. Young students are exposed to diverse pathways of connections and associations. They have the opportunity to read and engage in many different literature selections. The teacher supports their interests and helps to construct explicit connections for students. They also visit the theme through social studies, math, science, and art/music/drama activities. The classroom becomes a place where the ocean is all around, from pictures of the sea to stories about sea animals and experiments with salt water. Through an interdisciplinary approach to the curriculum, the students are immersed in the theme.

Sea Water Experiments

Sea animals live in sea water. Demonstrate these experiments for your class so they can see how sea water is different from the fresh water lakes or ponds students may have near their homes.

Experiment 1	Experiment 2	Experiment 3
How do we know that ocean and sea water contain salt? **Materials:** pie pan; 2 cups (480 mL) ocean or sea water (You can make your own by mixing 2 tsp [10 mL] of salt with 2 cups [480 mL] of water.) **Directions:** Pour the water into a pan. Place the pan in a warm, dry place. Allow water to evaporate—this usually takes a few days. Make observations.	Why does an iceberg float? **Materials:** a glass jar, water, a freezer, scale **Directions:** Fill the jar to the top with water. Weigh the jar of water. Carefully place the jar in the freezer. Close the freezer door; in three hours, observe what has taken place. Weigh the jar again and compare this weight with its pre-frozen weight.	Is it easier to float in the ocean or in fresh water? **Materials:** 1 egg, 1 jar filled with fresh water, 1 jar filled with ocean water (You can make your own by mixing 2 tsp [10 mL] of salt with 2 cups [480 mL] of water.) **Directions:** Put the egg in the jar of fresh water. Observe what happens. Put the egg in the jar of ocean water. Observe what happens.

Reprinted from TCM 254 Thematic Unit: Sea Animals, *Teacher Created Materials, 1993*

Concluding Remarks

Interdisciplinary teaching and learning is an approach that values the learning process. Students are provided the freedom to construct their own connections among ideas, in and out of the classroom. An interdisciplinary approach supports the perspective that knowledge acquisition is developed when students have opportunities to collaborate and work together, sharing and negotiating ideas and concepts. Students also have opportunities to develop the thematic unit by brainstorming and identifying topics and themes that hold interest. The teacher encourages students to embrace an array of skills and processes as they participate in various projects and activities. An interdisciplinary approach creates a meaningful and purposeful environment for students to link to each other, to content, and to human experiences (Smith & Johnson, 1994).

Assessment Issues for an Integrated Curriculum

Alternative Assessment Strategies

Integrating the curriculum and developing thematic units do not lend themselves to end-of-chapter tests and isolated exams on pieces of knowledge. Your students are not completing worksheets with single right answers. The interactional patterns are changing, and it is difficult to check off student responses when the discussion is engaging and insightful. The diverse connections students are constructing do not fit comfortably and easily on report cards and other traditional methods of reporting progress. With changes in the way the curriculum is being implemented, there are also changes in the assessment formats. Teachers are now faced with discovering new ways to assess their students' growth in knowledge and evaluate their own abilities to teach the concepts and skills. These new assessment methods integrate and complement the integrated curriculum approach.

Alternative assessment procedures are authentic in nature. They are based on what students actually do in a variety of contexts at different points throughout the instructional year (Ryan, 1994). They are

> With changes in the way the curriculum is being implemented, there are also changes in the assessment formats.

interested in the learning processes students engage in, including the ways in which knowledge is represented, reorganized, and used to process new information. Alternative assessment practices include such methods as portfolios, performance-based activities, running records, checklists, anecdotal records, observations, etc. With alternative assessment practices, evaluation is perceived as part of the ongoing daily experience in the classroom (Goodman, 1991).

Aligning assessment practices with curriculum and instruction creates in the students an awareness that what is taught and developed is assessed, and the information gained from the assessment is meaningful and will be utilized to inform future activities and projects (Seely, 1994). Integrated curriculum approaches to learning support the interrelated pathways between instruction and assessment. Your students are engaged in a variety of tasks, painting pictures of their thinking patterns and abilities. Through the many tasks and projects, you are able to determine the next step in instruction. Questions to consider asking may include:

> **Integrated curriculum approaches to learning support the interrelated pathways between instruction and assessment.**

◆ Does the student understand the concepts presented?

◆ Has the student been engaged in the learning process?

◆ Is the student making connections between the ideas and concepts presented in the different contexts?

◆ What pathways does the student seem to be following?

◆ What information does the student seem to be seeking?

These questions, among others, will help you develop activities and projects that address the needs of your students as they participate in integrated learning.

Portfolios

Portfolios have become a popular alternative assessment practice in many classrooms and fit nicely with integrated curriculum classrooms. Portfolios enable students and teachers to view the learning process through a collection of samples and artifacts. Paulson and Paulson (1991) have offered a substantive definition of portfolio assessment:

A purposeful, integrated collection of student work showing student effort, progress, or achievement in one or more areas. The collection is guided by performance standards and includes evidence of students' self-reflection and participation in setting the focus, selecting contents, and judging merit (p. 295).

Portfolios provide you and your students with evidence of growth and development as the pieces of information are evaluated. The process of collecting artifacts is a continuous one as new pieces are included and old pieces lose their relevance. Through the portfolios, learning is perceived as always evolving and changing. As with integrated curriculum approaches to learning and teaching, "portfolios offer opportunities for students and teachers to better understand the expansive nature of learning and assessment" (Seely, 1994, p.4).

There are a variety of portfolios that can be implemented into integrated curriculum classrooms. Portfolios serve many different purposes. "Depending on the tradition, the purpose, and the context, a portfolio may be evidence of one's own work, the work of others [in a cooperative group setting], solitary work, mentored work, best work, or all work (Collins, 1992, p. 452). The types of portfolios identified by Valencia and Calfee (1991) include showcase, documentation, and evaluation. In later work, the process portfolio was identified (Valencia & Place, in press). The documentation and process portfolios are the two most applicable for assessment in an integrated curriculum classroom.

> Through the portfolios, learning is perceived as always evolving and changing.

The documentation portfolio is a method of collecting students' work systematically over a period of time. The collection includes a wide variety of samples: rough drafts, brainstorming activities, math tasks and story problems, checklists, science activities, responses given in discussions, anecdotal notes, running records, etc. This portfolio enables work from all areas of the curriculum to be included. The parameters for the collection are defined by you and your students. Making decisions about what is significant and what is not is an important aspect of the documentation portfolio. Without some of this decision making, too many samples will be collected, leaving you and your students feeling overwhelmed.

The process portfolio is the newest type on the assessment scene. It is a portfolio of items and artifacts demonstrating work that is part of a larger project. The items are drawn from an integrated curriculum involving many tasks and activities. A process portfolio focuses on a student's progress in smaller increments of time. The advantage of implementing a process portfolio is that it enables teachers and students to have a more flexible curriculum, one based on need and interest.

Sample forms to consider for the documentation or process portfolios within an integrated curriculum are on pages 62 and 63. The forms are guidelines to help keep track of the students' work and progress as portfolios are implemented in your classroom.

Portfolio Requirements for a Thematic Classroom

Student Name: _____

Theme One:

_____ Reading _____

_____ Writing _____

_____ Math _____

_____ Social Studies _____

_____ Art/Music _____

_____ Other _____

Theme Two:

_____ Reading _____

_____ Writing _____

_____ Math _____

_____ Social Studies _____

_____ Art/Music _____

_____ Other _____

Theme Three:

_____ Reading _____

_____ Writing _____

_____ Math _____

_____ Social Studies _____

_____ Art/Music _____

_____ Other _____

Reprinted from TCM Workshop Notebook Portfolios and Other Alternative Assessments, *Teacher Created Materials, 1993*

What's in It?—Thematic Unit

Our Thematic Unit on _____

This portfolio contains the following items:

_____ Reading

_____ Writing

_____ Social Studies

_____ Science

_____ Art

_____ Music

_____ Other

_____ Student Reflection on Work

In addition to the guidelines for documenting and recording the students' work and progress, it is also important to consider the cooperative nature of integrated curriculum. Portfolios, for the most part, are records of individual student growth and development. In many cases, however, students in integrated curriculum classrooms are actively involved in collaborative projects. The collaborations range from small tasks, such as working on writing math problems together, to larger culminating activities where many students are working toward a common goal. How do students include these collaborations in their individual portfolios, and how does a teacher assess students as they work together to construct meaning? Photographs of the group projects are an excellent way of documenting the project. This way all participants in the project are able to have a representation of the project in their portfolios. Collaborative group projects ask your students to gain understandings involving more than the final results of the project. Students must also develop understandings of what it means to be part of a group and their roles within the group. Assessing their own participation in the group will encourage your students to be reflective of the process as well as the product. Students can complete reflective group forms, such as the one on the next page.

Portfolios play an integral role in alternative assessment practices. With the focus on learning moving from an isolated skills approach to an integrated, contextualized approach, portfolios offer teachers and students opportunities to expand views of assessment. Through portfolios, students and teachers are able to evaluate not only the product but also the learning processes involved. Portfolios enable students and teachers to have a glimpse of the pathways and avenues of learning in an integrated curriculum.

Portfolios, for the most part, are records of individual student growth and development.

Student Checklist
Cooperative Learning Groups

Name: _____ Activity: _____

Check off the following if you were a responsible group member:

_____ Followed directions carefully.

_____ Used a quiet voice when speaking.

_____ Knew my job in the group and did it.

_____ Stayed on task.

_____ Asked questions politely.

_____ Took turns politely.

_____ Encouraged others (no put downs).

_____ Was a good example for others.

_____ Contributed my best ideas and behavior to the group.

_____ Stayed with the group until the activity was complete.

Reprinted from TCM Workshop Notebook Portfolios and Other Alternative Assessments, *Teacher Created Materials, 1993*

Other Alternative Assessment Practices

In integrated curriculum classrooms, teachers also implement other forms of alternative assessment. Performance-based and observation-based assessment are two methods teachers are utilizing. Performance-based assessment involves documenting and assessing students as they solve realistic problems. It looks at prior knowledge, recent learning, and relevant skills as they apply this knowledge in various contexts and situations (Ryan, 1994). This type of assessment fits well with the beliefs and practices of integrated curriculum approaches to learning. Performance-based assessment values the different pathways to knowledge that students travel as they apply their skills to authentic and meaningful activities.

Performance-based assessment involves documenting and assessing students as they solve realistic problems.

With performance-based assessment practices, you are interested in the types of knowledge, declarative and procedural, as well as critical thinking skills students bring to the task. To assess this knowledge, your students may be engaged in a task addressing one of the following skills or concepts: comparing, contrasting, decision making, predicting, inventing, analyzing, and experimenting, among others. As they participate in the performance-based task, you are able to observe and evaluate their processes as well as the products.

Observation-based assessment is another method teachers are implementing to assess and evaluate student progress and achievement. Observation is not new to teachers, it is just becoming more systematic and purposeful. Observing students in a variety of contexts in a variety of situations is important to the validity of the assessment (Ryan, 1994). Observations enable you to view your students as they participate in activities and projects. An integrated curriculum approach provides teachers with a way to gain an authentic look at how their students are constructing the pathways of connections.

Types of observation notes include checklists and anecdotal records. Both are ways in which the teacher quietly records the behaviors and interactions of the students as they are engaged in tasks and activities. Anecdotal records are taken for a variety of reasons. You may want to observe a particular child or the entire class. It might be in one part of the day or another. Anecdotal notes enable teachers to reflect on the actions and behaviors of individual students or in certain projects. Checklists, on the other hand, are ways to record whether a certain task or concept was addressed. They do not judge or assess how well the task was performed, only that it was accomplished. The value of checklists is that they focus the observations and are helpful in identifying whether or not students need additional attention in certain areas.

Alternative assessment practices, such as performance and observation-based assessment, enable teachers and students to successfully integrate assessment and instruction. Bringing the two interrelated processes together supports integrated learning and thinking. Students have opportunities to utilize assessment as a tool for improving the instruction.

Reflection

Reflection is a critical and significant aspect of an integrated curriculum approach. Both students and teachers engage in the reflection process to better understand the complexities of the learning process. Reflection occurs throughout the thematic unit and after it is completed. "To examine the process, its value to students, and the learning outcomes, teachers [and students] must consistently assess what is actually happening against what was actually planned and expected" (Smith & Johnson, 1994, p. 207). Questions you may ask of yourself include:

◆ Is this a meaningful learning experience for my students?

◆ Are the activities and projects meeting the desired learning outcomes and objectives?

◆ What types of connections are students making that may impact future learning experiences?

◆ Was this thematic unit well organized and planned? What should I do differently next time?

◆ What expectations did I have for this unit? Were they met? If not, how might I alter the teaching to meet the expectations?

Through reflective thinking, pathways and avenues to knowledge are identified and acknowledged. You are then able to adapt and alter activities and projects to better meet the needs of the your students.

Students should also have the opportunity to reflect on their actions and progress in thematic units and integrated learning. Reflection allows your students to have a voice in the learning process. They are able to provide feedback and information to the teacher about the thematic unit and the connections they made while engaged in the learning process. Encouraging your students to participate in self-reflection will support and empower them. Reflection enables students to validate and justify the pathways of knowledge constructed.

> Reflection is a critical and significant aspect of an integrated curriculum approach.

The reflective process, for both students and teachers, ensures that teaching and learning are constantly evaluated in terms of their actual impact. You are enriched by the process because it helps focus the instruction and provides information on the effectiveness of different teaching strategies. Your students are enriched through reflection because it offers a place to voice their thinking about learning and their role in the process. Students become more engaged in learning when they believe they have input in the learning activities. Implementing reflective thinking into an integrated curriculum supports the notion that integrated learning is authentic and meaningful to students and teachers. Reflection, therefore, is an important part of the teaching and learning processes.

Concluding Remarks

Teachers and learners engage in informal reflection every time they analyze and wonder about the lesson.

Alternative assessment and reflection play an integral part in the success of an integrated curriculum. Assessment in an integrated curriculum classroom does not easily follow the traditional methods used for evaluation. Students are actively engaged in many projects for different purposes. Alternative assessment practices align themselves with these different purposes and projects. Common alternative assessment practices include portfolios and performance-based and observation-based assessment. Your students and you have a large role in determining the samples of work to be collected for portfolios and the application of skills in performance-based and observation-based assessments. The strength of alternative assessment practices as they relate to integrated curriculum approaches lies in the ability to interrelate and connect to the outcomes and objectives of the curriculum and thematic units.

Reflection is an aspect that is often not addressed in a formal manner. Teachers and learners engage in informal reflection every time they analyze and wonder about the lesson. Through reflection, students and teachers are able to gain a better understanding of the concepts presented and of the learning process. Reflective thinking offers you and your students opportunities to voice thinking patterns, thereby supporting a meaningful and purposeful curriculum.

These two areas, alternative assessment and reflection, provide an integrated curriculum with avenues to fully complete the learning process. Incorporating alternative assessment and reflection into the learning and thinking of students and teachers creates opportunities for links and connections to other themes and to the world outside the classroom doors.

Bringing It All Together

Finishing Touches

In previous chapters you were exposed to many aspects and features of integrated learning and integrated curriculums. Throughout each chapter different areas and issues have been explored. As you read the chapters and began thinking about your own classroom, connections and links were beginning to form. Perhaps an idea caught your attention because you were already familiar with it, or perhaps your attention was captured because you had never encountered such an idea or perspective. Either way, you were utilizing your background knowledge and experiences to make connections. Developing connections enables you to process new information and begin to understand new concepts and perspectives. With these connections you are able to gain understandings about events in the world.

The connections you constructed as you began to piece together the ideas from this book are similar to the process students use when faced with an integrated curriculum. Integrated curriculum approaches provide students with opportunities to make the explicit connections needed to better understand ideas and concepts in and

> Developing connections enables you to process new information and begin to understand new concepts and perspectives.

out of the classroom environment. These connections are constructed in many different ways for many different purposes. Student bring to activities and projects their own thinking patterns. Through negotiations meanings are shaped and reshaped, providing students with new interpretations. The explicitness of the connections in an integrated curriculum encourages students to view learning as a process with many different pathways and avenues.

Throughout the chapters many points were identified and addressed to further understanding of the integrated learning and integrated curriculum approaches. The connections to the theme of integrated curriculum are diverse. A historical connection was introduced early on to provide a background for how an integrated curriculum was started. In the days of Dewey and the progressive education movement, integrated learning was the pinnacle of effective and purposeful learning. Dewey believed that students construct their own meaning through questions and curiosities. Having opportunities to exploit their questions and engage in purposeful learning is the nature of integrated learning. It is authentic and relevant to the lives of students in and out of the classroom environment. The resurgence of Dewey's ideas has made an impact in many classrooms. Social constructive thinking is influencing the way teachers and students perceive learning and development. Learning is seen as occurring in social contexts where knowledge is shared and negotiated, creating new interpretations of the world around us. Teachers are also beginning to implement integrated curriculums with students who come from culturally diverse backgrounds. Integrated curriculum approaches enable students to construct their own thinking patterns based on diverse representations of the world.

> There are features of the classroom environment critical to supporting practices and beliefs of integrated curriculum.

With the historical perspective in place, the role of the classroom environment provides a way for you to implement the ideas of integrated curriculum and integrated learning. There are features of the classroom environment critical to supporting practices and beliefs of integrated curriculum. Opportunities for your students to work in cooperative groups, to engage in alternative interactional patterns, including discussions, peer talking, and partner sharing, are characteristics familiar to integrated curriculum classrooms. Additionally, opportunities for you to have flexibility in the planning and implementing of the curriculum, to have solid understandings of the skills and concepts, and to be a reflective teacher and researcher promote the use of integrated curriculums in the classroom. From these opportunities the classroom environment becomes important to the success of integrated curriculum approaches to learning.

Now that ideas about implementing an integrated curriculum in your own classroom are in the forefront of your thinking, the beginning steps to integration are critical to the success of the approach. This is the action-oriented perspective. Beginning steps include looking for appropriate themes and deciding on the criteria for selection and ways to restructure your instructional day to best meet the needs of integrating the curriculum. Themes are best explored when both the students and teacher have voices in offering suggestions. The use of thematic webs helps in brainstorming and organizing the information. Restructuring the instructional day to include larger blocks of time supports the notion that integrated learning is more than forty minutes of decontextualized, isolated skill building. Given the additional time, the extending blocks encourage students to make connections and links between and among different disciplines.

To help make these ideas more salient, two approaches to integrated curriculum are intradisciplinary and interdisciplinary. The intradisciplinary approach integrates ideas and concepts in one discipline. In most cases this integration occurs in language arts. Reading and writing activities are good places to begin understanding the interconnected relationship between processes and concepts.

Reading and writing activities are good places to begin understanding the interconnected relationship between processes and concepts.

The interdisciplinary approach to the curriculum is more involved than the intradisciplinary. In this approach, all of the disciplines are integrated. There is an overall theme that is the focus of the integration. As these connections and links are made, new and diverse pathways and avenues of thinking emerge. Students will offer new interpretations to old information. The importance of highlighting and supporting the connections made is that without the connections, learning becomes an isolated, decontextualized event. Interdisciplinary approaches to the curriculum are challenging, to say the least. They require effort, planning, and organizing the many samples of information. It is an approach, however, that offers the "window to the world." Integrating the curriculum is exciting and engaging.

Finally, the issues of assessment and reflection are addressed as you bring the integrated curriculum approach to a close. Alternative assessment practices are aligned with the philosophy of integrated curriculums. Within alternative assessment, portfolios and performance-based and observation-based assessment, it is possible to gain insight into the thinking patterns of the students. Insights also occur as teachers and students engage in reflective thinking. Reflection offers opportunities to focus the learning and evaluate the strengths and weaknesses of lessons and teaching strategies.

Recall the imagined scene where students were actively engaged in a variety of tasks and projects, and the teacher was helping to facilitate knowledge and understandings. In this scene, teachers and students are constructing connections and links to pathways of knowledge. As new knowledge is integrated and shared with other teachers or students, it is important to recognize the diversity among students, disciplines, and connections. An integrated curriculum is one that is beginning to make some headway into the ways in which learning and knowledge are developed. Connections are created, "represent[ing] a way to avoid the fragmented and irrelevant acquisition of isolated facts, transforming knowledge into personally useful tools for learning new information" (Lipson, Valencia, Wixon, & Peters, 1993, p. 252). Taking the initial steps and noticing the strengths of an integrated curriculum enables you and your students to begin to build roads to learning and thinking. To conclude, a quote from the delightful tale, *Seven Blind Mice* (Young, 1992), sums up the philosophy and perspective offered by integrated learning and teaching, "knowing in part may make a fine tale, but wisdom comes from seeing the whole."

References

Allington, R. (1994). Reducing the risk: Integrated language arts in restructured elementary schools. In L. Morrow, J. Smith, & L. Wilkinson (Eds.), <u>Integrated language arts: Controversy to consensus</u> (pp. 193–213). Needham Heights, MA: Allyn and Bacon.

Applebee, A. (1991). Environments for language teaching and learning: Contemporary issues and future directions. In J. Flood, J. M. Jensen, D. Lapp, & J. Squire (Eds.), <u>Handbook of research on teaching the English language arts</u> (pp. 554–556). New York: Macmillan.

Britton, J. (1993). <u>Language and learning</u>. Portsmouth, NH: Heinemann.

Brophy, J., & Alleman, J. (1991). A caveat: Curriculum integration isn't always a good idea. <u>Educational Leadership, 49</u>(2), 66.

Bruner, J. (1986). <u>Actual minds, possible worlds</u>. Cambridge, MA: Harvard University Press.

Carle, E. (1967). <u>The very hungry caterpillar</u>. New York: Philomel.

Carle, E. (1987). <u>A house for hermit crab</u>. New York: Scholastic.

Casteel, C., & Isom, B. (1994). Reciprocal processes in science and literacy learning. <u>The Reading Teacher, 47</u>, 538–545.

Cazden, C. (1988). <u>Classroom discourse: The language of teaching and learning</u>. Portsmouth, NH: Heinemann.

Collins, A. (1992). Portfolios for science education. Issues in purpose, structure, and authenticity. <u>Science Education, 76, 451</u>–463.

Cornbleth, C. (1990). <u>Curriculum in context</u>. Bristol, PA: Falmer Press.

Dewey, J. (1933). <u>How we think</u>. Boston, MA: Heath.

Dewey, J., & Childs, J. (1933). The underlying philosophy of education. In W. Kilpatrick, B. Bode, J. Dewey, J. Childs, R. Raup, H. Hullfish, & V. Thayer (Eds.), <u>The educational frontier</u> (pp. 287–319). New York: Appleton-Century Company.

Dorros, A. (1990). <u>Rain forest secrets</u>. New York: Scholastic.

Dyson, A. H. (1993). <u>Social worlds of children learning to write</u>. New York: Teachers College Press.

Dyson, A. H. (1995). Writing children: Reinventing the development of childhood literacy. <u>Written Communication 12</u>(1) 4–46.

Fogarty, R. (1991). Ten ways to integrate curriculum. <u>Educational Leadership, 49</u>(2), 61–65.

Fritz, J. (1987). <u>Shh! We're writing the Constitution</u>. New York: Putnam.

Gamberg, R., Kwak, W., Hutchings, M., & Altheim, J. (1988). <u>Learning and loving it: Theme studies in the classroom</u>. Portsmouth, NH: Heinemann.

George, J. (1990). <u>One day in the tropical rain forest</u>. New York: Crowell.

Good, H. (1956). <u>The history of American education</u>. New York: Macmillan.

Goodman, K. (1989). Whole language is whole: A response to Heymsfeld. <u>Educational Leadership, 46</u>(6), 69–70.

Goodman, Y. (1991). Informal methods of evaluation. In J. Flood, J. Jenson, D. Lapp, & J. Squire (Eds.), <u>Handbook of research on the teaching of the English language arts</u> (pp. 502–509). New York: Macmillan.

References *(cont.)*

Graham, B. (1993). New directions in portfolio assessment: Assessing the assessor. (Report No. 143). Winnepeg, Canada. (ERIC Document Reproduction Service No. ED 355 537).

Hartman, D. (1994). The intertextual links of readers using multiple passages: A postmodern/semiotic/cognitive view of meaning making. In R. Ruddell, M. Ruddell, & H. Singer (Eds.), Theoretical models and processes of reading (pp. 616–636). Newark, DE: International Reading Association.

Heath, S. (1983). Ways with words: Language, life and work in communities and classrooms. Cambridge, MA: Cambridge University Press.

Heimlich, J., & Pittelman, S. (1990). Semantic mapping: Classroom application. Newark, DE: International Reading Association.

Henderson, J. (1992). Reflective teaching: Becoming an inquiring educator. New York: Macmillan.

Hullfish, H. (1933). The school: Its tasks and its administration. In W. Kilpatrick, B. Bode, J. Dewey, J. Childs, R. Raup, H. Hullfish, & V. Thayer (Eds.), The educational frontier (pp. 160–192). New York: Appleton-Century Company.

Lapp, D., & Flood, J. (1994). Integrating the curriculum: First steps. The Reading Teacher, 47, 416–419.

Lawson, R. (1988). Ben and me. Boston, MA: Little, Brown.

Leal, D. (1993). The power of literary peer-group discussions: How children collaboratively negotiate meaning. The Reading Teacher, 47, 114–121.

Levy, E. (1987). If you were there when they signed the Constitution. New York: Scholastic.

Lionni, L. (1963). Swimmy. New York: Scholastic.

Lipson, M., Valencia, S., Wixon, K., & Peters, C. (1993). Integration and thematic teaching: Integration to improve teaching and learning. Language Arts, 70, 252–263.

Marshak, S. (1991). I am the ocean. Boston, MA: Little, Brown.

Mehan, H. (1979). Learning lessons. Cambridge, MA: Harvard University Press.

Newkirk, T. (1991). The middle class and the problem of pleasure. In N. Atwell (Ed.), Workshop 3: The politics of process (pp. 63–72). Portsmouth, NH: Heinemann.

Nieto, S. (1992). Affirming diversity: The sociopolitical context of multicultural education. White Plains, New York: Longman.

Oldfather, P. (1993). What students say about motivating experiences in a whole language classroom. The Reading Teacher, 46, 672–681.

Pappas, C., Kiefer, B., & Levstick, L. (1995). An integrated language perspective in the elementary school. White Plains, NY: Longman.

Paulson, P. R., & Paulson, F. L. (1991). Portfolios: Stories of knowing. In P. Dreyer (Ed.), Knowing: The power of stories (pp. 294–303). Claremont, CA: Claremont Reading Conference.

References *(cont.)*

Pearson, P. D. (1994). Integrated language arts: Sources of controversy, seeds of consensus. In L. Morrow, J. Smith, & L. Wilkinson (Eds.), Integrated language arts: Controversy to consensus (pp. 11–32). Needham Heights, MA: Allyn & Bacon.

Peet, B. (1970). The wump world. Boston, MA: Houghton Mifflin.

Podendorf, I. (1982). Animals of sea and shore. Chicago: Children's Press.

Rand, M. (1994). Using thematic instruction to organize an integrated language arts classroom. In L. Morrow, J. Smith, & L. Wilkinson (Eds.), Integrated language arts: Controversy to consensus (pp. 177–192). Needham Heights, MA: Allyn & Bacon.

Raphael, T., & McMahon, S. (1994). Book club: An alternative framework for reading instruction. The Reading Teacher, 48, 102–116.

Rogoff, B. (1990). Apprenticeship in thinking. New York: Oxford University Press.

Rosenblatt, L. (1994). The transactional theory of reading and writing. In R. Ruddell, M. Ruddell, & H. Singer (Eds.), Theoretical models and processes of reading (pp. 1057–1092). Newark, DE: International Reading Association.

Routman, R. (1991). Invitations: Changing as teachers and learners, K–12. Portsmouth, NH: Heinemann.

Ryan, C. (1994). Authentic assessment. Westminster, CA: Teacher Created Materials.

Seely, A. (1994). Portfolio assessment. Westminster, CA: Teacher Created Materials.

Sheldon, D. (1991). The whale's song. New York: Dial Books.

Shubert, B. (1993). Literacy: What makes it real? Integrated thematic teaching. Social Studies Review, 32(2), 7–16.

Smith, J., & Johnson, H. (1994). Models for implementing literature in content studies. The Reading Teacher, 48, 198–209.

Spier, P. (1987). We the people: The Constitution of the United States of America. New York: Doubleday.

Stevenson, C., & Carr, J. (1993). Goals for integrated studies. In C. Stevenson, & J. Carr (Eds.), Integrated studies in the middle grades: Dancing through walls (pp. 7–25). New York: Teachers College Press.

Thayer, V. (1933). The school: Its tasks and its administration—III. In W. Kilpatrick, B. Bode, J. Dewey, J. Childs, R. Raup, H. Hullfish, & V. Thayer (Eds.), The educational frontier (pp. 213–256). New York: Appleton-Century Company.

U. S. Department of Education. (1993, February). Adjusted national estimated data from an elementary and secondary school civil rights survey—1990. Washington, DC: U. S. Office for Civil Rights.

Valencia, S., & Calfee, R. (1991). The development and use of literacy portfolios for students, classes, and teachers. Applied Measurement in Education, 4, 333–345.

Valencia, S., & Place, N. (in press). A study of literacy portfolios for teaching, learning, and accountability.

References *(cont.)*

Van Allsburg, C. (1990). <u>Just a dream</u>. Boston, MA: Houghton Mifflin.

Vygotsky, L. (1978). <u>Mind in society</u>. Cambridge, MA: Harvard University Press.

Whitfield, P. (1991). <u>Oceans</u>. New York: Viking.

Winograd, K., & Higgins, K. (1994). Writing, reading, and talking mathematics: One interdisciplinary possibility. <u>The Reading Teacher, 48</u>, 310–318.

Young, E. (1992). <u>Seven blind mice</u>. New York: Scholastic.

Teacher Created Materials Reference List

TCM #286 Thematic Unit: Ecology
TCM #254 Thematic Unit: Sea Animals
TCM #582 Thematic Unit: U.S. Constitution

TCM Workshop Notebook "Portfolios and Other Alternative Assessments"

Other Teacher Created Materials Thematic Unit Resources

Primary
TCM #249 Thematic Unit: Tide Pools and Coral Reefs
TCM #267 Thematic Unit: Bears
TCM #276 Thematic Unit: Native Americans

Intermediate
TCM #230 Thematic Unit: Multicultural Folk Tales
TCM #236 Thematic Unit: Electricity
TCM #239 Thematic Unit: Chocolate

Challenging
TCM #290 Thematic Unit: Civil War
TCM #292 Thematic Unit: Ancient Egypt
TCM #590 Thematic Unit: African Americans